Harwich

Hook of Holland
1893-2020

Ferry
Publications

Published by:
Ferry Publications,
PO Box 33,
Ramsey,
Isle of Man IM99 4LP
Tel: +44 (0) 1624 898445
E-mail: sales@lilypublications.co.uk
Website: www.ferrypubs.co.uk

John Hendy Miles Cowsill Stephen Brown

Contents

First Published: June 2010
Revised and update edition: June 2020

Acknowledgements

The publishers would like to thank Henk van der Lugt for assistance with this publication, especially for his wealth of knowledge in relation to SMZ and the Hook of Holland. The authors would also like to thank the following for their input to the book with information and photographs: Wirral Archives, Rob de Visser, Ian Boyle, GR van Veldhoven, John Bryant and FotoFlite.

Dedication

The authors would like to dedicate this new edition to the late Pim de Lange, former Managing Director of Stena Line BV, who gave us so much support and encouragement over the years with our interest in shipping and this famous link.

Introduction

This is the third book that Ferry Publications has produced concerning the historic link between Harwich and the Hook of Holland.

The Great Eastern Railway opened the service to Rotterdam in 1863 with chartered tonnage carrying mainly cattle before introducing their first vessel, the paddle steamer *Avalon* in the following year. The early service was forced to negotiate the treacherous waters of the Maas (Rhine) estuary and groundings in the ever-changing delta caused frequent problems. This was overcome in 1872 with the opening of the New Waterway which saved the port of Rotterdam and enabled ships of any size to reach a safe haven from the open sea at any state of the tide. Under the great Dutch engineer Caland, work on this ambitious project had commenced in 1866 and in March 1872, the Great Eastern's paddle steamer *Richard Young* became the first vessel to use it on her journey to Rotterdam Parkkade.

On the English side, a new and spacious Harwich terminal was built for the Great Eastern in 1879. It was named Parkeston Quay in honour of the GER's Chairman Charles Parkes and opened in February 1883. Although two miles further upriver from Harwich, the new £500,000 facilities allowed for tremendous growth and development.

The construction of the New Waterway also opened up a new port at the Hook of Holland in June 1893, the GER's *Chelmsford* opening the new quay. This allowed passengers to disembark and save time by travelling to Rotterdam by train while the steamers continued into the city to unload cargo. It was not until 1903 that the Rotterdam service ceased.

With the Great Eastern Railway being absorbed into the London & North Eastern Railway (LNER) in 1923 came new ships and an improvement in the through service between London and Rotterdam/Amsterdam. Then in 1948, the railway companies in the UK were nationalised and the LNER became British Railways, a state of affairs that lasted until the denationalisation of Sealink UK Ltd in 1984.

Dutch participation on the route had started in 1947. During that year the SMZ (Zeeland Steamship Company) switched its daily service from its base at Vlissingen to the Hook of Holland although Harwich had superceded Folkestone as its English terminal in 1927.

With the British ships offering night sailings and the Dutch vessels operating by day, this situation continued until 1968 when the joint car ferry service was introduced. Further changes occurred when in June 1989, Stena Line of Sweden acquired SMZ and in April 1990 also took control of the British Sealink operation. At this time the management of the route passed to Dutch control through the subsidiary Stena BV.

Much has happened throughout the fascinating history of the route. It is a story of endeavour, social change and technological advance, of triumph and tragedy both in war and in peace and, above all, it is a story of the ships. Today universally known as 'ferries', the vessels that have linked England and the Netherlands, across the southern North Sea, have changed beyond all recognition.

Since taking over the route, Stena Line BV have shown that they are fully committed to continuing the development of ports, the route and its ships. The introduction of the world's largest passenger/vehicle ferries in 2010 is most certainly the most confident seal of approval that any shipping company could give. Today's strength and confidence is built upon the solid foundations of the past and the old publicity slogan 'Harwich for the Continent' is as true now as it ever was.

A view of Parkeston Quay in the twenties from the port's Christmas card in 1992. (Stena Line)

CHAPTER ONE

The Early Days

The Eastern Counties Railways Company reached the town of Harwich in August 1854 and it was not long before other enterprising concerns were attempting to extend the line's sphere of influence to the Continental ports of Rotterdam, Antwerp and Hamburg.

The most successful of these independent ventures was the service started on 16th September 1854 by the North of Europe Steam Navigation Company when the paddle steamer *Aquila* set out for Antwerp. The company eventually folded in February 1858 but four-and-a-half years later the amalgamation of a number of East Anglian railway companies led to the formation of the Great Eastern Railway, which in 1863 gained power to operate their own ships from the port of Harwich.

On 3rd October that year, the chartered *Blenheim* sailed from Rotterdam with a cargo of cattle and the following months saw the *Norfolk* and *Prince of Wales* enter service.

Charter arrangements were never satisfactory, being both costly and unreliable, and so the Great Eastern's Directors lost little time in ordering their own tonnage from J & W Dudgeon of London.

The first vessel was the paddle steamer *Avalon* which commenced her 13-hour service to Rotterdam on 13th June 1864 while her sister *Zealous* opened the weekly Antwerp link on 1st August.

Conditions on board these early steamers were extremely spartan. The bar included a pantry, while adjacent to this a large open saloon contained wooden tables and comfortable seats. Around the outside of the saloon, curtained off from the main area, were alcoves in which were fitted twin bunks. Regarded as a very luxurious ship for her time, the *Avalon* accommodated as many as 115 passengers.

Until the outbreak of World War 1 the main cargo carried was cattle for the meat trade although, until the New Waterway was opened in 1872, Rotterdam was approached in a vastly different way from today. The old channels used in the approaches to the Dutch port were silting up, although the Voornsche Canal (built in 1829) enabled larger ships to approach from the south west. Even this was not adequate as the size of ships was rapidly increasing.

SEAWAYS TO ROTTERDAM

In the first quarter of the nineteenth century Rotterdam's status as a port was equalled by that of Antwerp (then, before the founding of Belgium, part of the Greater Netherlands) but neither approached the importance of Amsterdam. However, it was becoming essential for Rotterdam to expand as the vast natural

The iron-hulled paddle steamer **Harwich** *was one of the Great Eastern's first vessels for the Rotterdam link.*

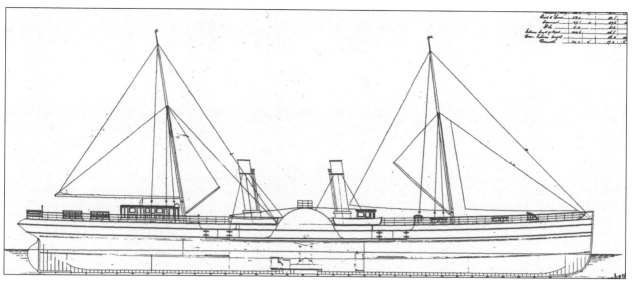

*The **Claud Hamilton** entered service in 1875 and was highly regarded by her crews and the general public. She remained in service until 1897. (Strathclyde Regional Archives)*

hinterland of the Rhine valley badly needed an outlet through which to export the region's wealth.

In 1816 the first steamship arrived in the port and the draft of ships continued to increase during a time when the waters of the Rhine and Maas deltas were continuing to be filled with deposits of mud, sand and silt.

The original approach to Rotterdam from the sea was by way of the old exit of the River Maas through the Brielsche Gap and by way of Botlek and the New Maas. Ships frequently grounded and to avoid this a longer but deeper channel through the Goereesche Gap, by way of Haringvlier, Hollands Diep, Dordtse Kil, the Old Maas, Botlek and the New Maas was used.

As early as the eighteenth century the Dutch engineer

Nicolaas Cruquius had devised a plan to pierce the coastline near to the Hook of Holland, thereby creating a straight cut between Rotterdam and the North Sea, although it was to take over a century-and-a-half to see this ambitious plan realised.

It was the 'King-merchant', King Willem I (1813-1840), who gave the order and provided the finances to construct the Voornsche Canal which was finally opened in 1829. This was a great step forward and for ten years provided a safe and well-used passage to Rotterdam. However, after about 1840 when trade began to develop and expand with the Dutch East Indies, the Voornsche Canal was found wanting and, in order to reduce their draft, large vessels would frequently discharge much of

*The **Lady Tyler** was built at North Shields in 1880 but served only the briefest of careers. (Ferry Publications Library)*

their cargo into smaller ships before attempting to enter the maze of channels in the approaches to Rotterdam. At that time the passage through the estuary from Brouwershaven, passing outside the island of Flakkee and through the Voornsche Canal to Rotterdam, could take weeks, the port's reputation was at an all-time low and Antwerp reaped the benefits.

Mindful of the trade being lost, the Dutch Government engaged in long consultations about how to relieve Rotterdam's plight and the young engineer Pieter Caland proved to be its saviour.

Caland suggested that a new cut should be built from Rotterdam to the Hook of Holland and through the sand dunes into the North Sea. A narrow opening, Caland reasoned, would be sufficient as the tidal flow would serve to scour the entrance which in time would widen itself.

The Royal Consent was given by King Willem III on 24th January 1863 and work commenced during August. On 31st October 1866, the Prince of Orange cut the first sod and the sea was reached on 26th November two years later.

Until the time that the Hook of Holland was opened, the ships from Harwich used the Oosterkade opposite the railway station of the Netherlands Rhine Railway Company (NRS). Passengers could walk from the ship to their trains, although in the early days there do not appear to have been any special boat trains.

In 1877 the railway bridge was opened across the new New Maas and, as they were unable to pass beneath it, the ships were forced to use a new berth just down river from the station at the Westerkade and later the Parkkade. The all-important rail connection now required the use of a horse-drawn carriage or tram and this inconvenience made the development at the Hook of Holland, where transfer between ship and train was so swift, all the more important.

The construction of the New Waterway saved Rotterdam and enabled ships of any size to approach what is today the world's largest port.

A degree of uncertainty clouds the history of the Great Eastern's first *Avalon*. It appears that she was constructed to her builder's specifications yet failed to meet the Directors' expectations.

After the briefest service, she grounded on one of the numerous sandbanks in the approaches to Rotterdam and damaged herself to such an extent that she was sold back to Dudgeon's who, in turn, disposed of her to Brazil in February 1866.

The *Zealous* meanwhile was retained and was later given a new lease of life when she was re-boilered in 1873, thereby extending her career by another fourteen years.

Two other ships also entered service during 1864, these being the *Harwich* and the *Rotterdam* which were also built on the Thames. They were mainly cattle carriers which some twenty years later were sent to Messrs. Earle's yard at Hull for conversion to screw propulsion, after which the *Rotterdam* emerged with the name *Peterboro*. Both ships had long careers and remained in service well after the turn of the century.

On the stocks at Dudgeon's at the time when the

Great Eastern's Directors decided to part with the unsuccessful *Avalon* was a fifth ship. It has been suggested that the new vessel was to be named *Ravensbury*, but she was delivered in 1865 as the second-named *Avalon*.

Her sister was the *Ravensbury*, another ship which sadly enjoyed only the briefest of careers. As she was nearing Rotterdam on 8th March 1870, she grounded, sprung a leak and flooded. The vessel was abandoned and disappeared in the mud and silt of the River Maas.

During 1971 work was under way dredging in the Maasvlakte when an unnamed ship was discovered. In an effort to identify her, the dredging crew lifted half of the wreck, exposing square steam boilers, two oscillating engines and paddles with wooden blades. The vessel was finally identified by the discovery of a china wash-basin on which was painted the coat of arms of the Great Eastern Railway Company, although, unfortunately, pressure of time did not make possible a complete search before the wreck was reburied.

The year-old *Pacific* had been purchased in 1865 and yet further evidence of the route's growth occurred a year later when the cargo vessel *Yarmouth* joined the service.

Delivered from Dudgeon of London in 1871 was the *Richard Young*, which later gained fame when she became the first steamer to pass through the New Waterway on 9th March 1872.

THE NEW WATERWAY

The official opening of the New Waterway occurred ten days later but there was still much to be achieved. The *Richard Young* had only managed to enter the new cut at high water and enough time had not elapsed to encourage the expected tidal scouring. In time, the mud and sand being carried out by the tide actually started to accumulate in the narrow entrance, just before the channel widened, and a new bar began to build. For a while, vessels once more were forced to use the old Voornsche Canal at low water and, with larger ships and associated traffic increases, it was almost a case of going back to square one. By the end of 1872 only 416 ships had used the New Waterway and Caland's estimate of 5 million Guilders for its construction had doubled.

Frustrated and discouraged, Caland resigned and the engineer Willem Leemans was given the task of freeing the New Waterway and the port of Rotterdam. The great sand bar in the entrance was duly dredged and the fairway was widened and deepened. Although the accumulation of material is a never-ending story, its clearance allowed Rotterdam once more to become a leading port.

The great advantage of the New Waterway so far as the Harwich steamers were concerned was that for the first time the presence of a deep-water channel right into the heart to Rotterdam enabled them to operate a fixed, rather than a tidal, timetable as they no longer had to wait off the Dutch coast for sufficient water to cross the Brielle Bar.

However, there were those who were still concerned about possible delays to passenger ships on the New Waterway and the idea was mooted of a railway line from Rotterdam linking with the Hook of Holland. At this point a quay could be constructed alongside which the steamers could discharge their passengers into waiting trains. Up to two hours could be saved, the route would become more popular with the public and there was less chance of being held up by other shipping movements in the busier waters close to the city. This important time factor would also aid the transport of perishable goods such as fruit, vegetables and fish.

A CLYDE SHIP

Without doubt, the most notable of all the Great Eastern's paddle steamers was the *Claud Hamilton* which was named after the Company Chairman of the period. The order for the new steamer went to Scotland and to the River Clyde where John Elder & Company (later Fairfield of Govan) launched her on 3rd June 1875. In the same month the service to Rotterdam became daily.

Boasting a gross tonnage of almost 1,000, the *Claud Hamilton*'s size and reliability did much to improve the service and this fine paddler remained on station until 1897 as the last paddle steamer in the Great Eastern Railway's Continental fleet. Sold to the Corporation of London, she then served until 1914 carrying cattle between Gravesend and Deptford – a sad end for a notable ship.

During the summer of 1875, Stoomvaart Maatschappij Zeeland (SMZ), the Zeeland Steamship Company, was founded to operate a service between Flushing and Queenborough, on the Isle of Sheppey, in Kent. A night service was originally operated and was aided by good railway connections on both sides of the North Sea. The rival route caused the Great Eastern Railway much consternation and Hudig & Pieters, their agents in Rotterdam, wrote to the Dutch Government stating that unless a railway line between Rotterdam and

the Hook of Holland was constructed, they were sure that the Great Eastern would not only move their service away from Rotterdam but also from Holland.

A second Clyde-built steamer was the *Princess of Wales* of 1878. Capable of accommodating 580 passengers in two classes, the ship lasted until 1895.

Until now, the Great Eastern's Continental steamers had used the rather restricted Continental Pier at Harwich, opposite which was the thriving Great Eastern Hotel. However, a continuing disagreement between Harwich Town Council and the railway company ended with the latter taking rather drastic measures.

In January 1879, a contract was signed to build 1,000 yards of quays some two miles up river from Harwich on an area of saltings and mud-banks known locally as Ray Island. In this bleak and damp wilderness was then built accommodation for six vessels, plus moorings for an extra seven, offshore in the River Stour.

The difference between the space now created and the cramped conditions experienced back at Harwich was enormous, and it was not long before other shipping companies began expressing interest in the new facilities which also consisted of a new hotel, railway station and associated warehouses.

The new quay was named after Mr. Charles H Parkes, the Chairman of the Great Eastern Railway, and was officially opened on 15th February 1883. Parkeston Quay cost in the region of £500,000 and so infuriated Harwich that when the railway later sought to extend their quay in the town's direction, permission was refused.

The final two paddle steamers for the route were the *Lady Tyler* and the *Adelaide* which had appeared in 1880. The first was built at North Shields and entered service in May. With accommodation for about 700 passengers, she served an uneventful life before being disposed of in 1893

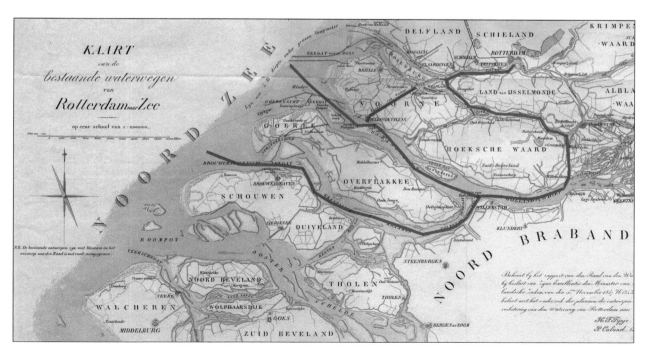

Map showing the various fairways from Rotterdam to the sea before the New Waterway was opened. The first seagoing vessel to pass through this new fairway on 9th March 1872 happened to be Great Eastern Railway's **Richard Young**. *The path of the New Waterway is indicated at the top of the map between Delfland and Voorne.*

Top: *The final Great Eastern paddle steamer to be built was the* **Adelaide** *in 1880. (G E Langmuir collection)*

Above: *The first screw steamers for the passenger operations were the* **Ipswich** *and* **Norwich** *of 1883. The* **Norwich** *seen here pictured in the River Stour. (G E Langmuir collection)*

Right: *The Great Eastern's turbine steamer* **St. Petersburg** *was launched at Clydebank in April 1910. She was renamed* **Archangel** *in 1919 and restarted the Hook service after the Great War with the* **Amsterdam**. *(Ferry Publications Library)*

*Another view of the first screw steamer the **Norwich** of 1883, seen at the Continental Pier, Harwich, in 1899. (G.E. Langmuir collection)*

as part payment for the new ship, *Chelmsford*. The second vessel was built at Barrow and was the first ship on the service constructed of steel. Like the *Lady Tyler*, her career was short – developments in ship construction and marine engineering bringing them to a premature demise.

SCREW SHIPS

Earle's of Hull had enjoyed increasing patronage from the Great Eastern and they were now rewarded by the order of a pair of reciprocating screw steamers intended to cope with the expected increase in traffic following the opening of Parkeston Quay.

The iron-hulled sisters very much set the trend for the remainder of the ships built for the Victorian fleet, although each of the subsequent vessels was a modified and enlarged version of the basic design.

Not only were the *Ipswich* and the *Norwich* the first reciprocating steamers for the Continental service but they were the first to carry local names served. They were launched in March and May 1883 and entered service in July and October. Their accommodation was for 84 in the First Class and 42 in the Second. Gross tonnage was 1,065 and dimensions were 260 ft. by 31 ft.. Service speed was about 14 knots although, as the crossing was by night, high speeds were never required, as little was gained by arriving at the port either too early or too long before the timetabled departure of the connecting trains.

As all the Great Eastern ships boasted comfortable cabin space, it was not surprising that on their demise Continental shipping companies should snap them up for further trading. Both the *Ipswich* and the *Norwich* were reboilered in the mid-1890s and remained in work until 1905 when they were sold to India and Portugal respectively. The former *Norwich* later crossed the Atlantic

Ocean to Argentina before ending her operating days in Mexico.

The next pair of steamers were 20 feet longer than the original pair and were constructed of steel. The *Cambridge* was launched in October 1886 while the *Colchester* followed three years later. As many as 730 passengers in two classes were carried and although they both commenced their careers on the Antwerp route, they were both soon switched to the Rotterdam link. These new ships saw off the ageing paddle steamers *Zealous* and *Pacific* and whereas the *Cambridge* remained in service until November 1911 (before being sold to Turkey and finally being scrapped in 1937 – her 51st year), the *Colchester* was not so fortunate.

A single ship, the *Chelmsford*, followed and was some 20 feet longer than the previous twins with a gross tonnage of 1,635. She was launched on 21st February 1893 and entered service four months later to coincide with the opening of the new port at the Hook of Holland.

HOOK OF HOLLAND

The long-awaited railway duly arrived at the Hook of Holland on 28th May 1893 and on the previous day over a hundred gentlemen of the press gathered at Parkeston Quay after their arrival by train from London (Liverpool Street). They were shown aboard the new *Chelmsford* which shortly afterwards embarked on a six-hour cruise and they could not have failed to be impressed with her interior which was finished in maple and satinwood. On the return to Parkeston Quay, the Great Eastern's Continental Traffic Manager, Mr. Gooday, invited all the crew to join him in a celebration dinner.

On 1st June the opening ceremony took place at the Hook of Holland. The *Chelmsford* duly arrived thirty minutes early at 05.30 and disembarked her passengers before

*The **Amsterdam** is seen here moored on the buoys in the River Stour with her raised bridge, which was fitted later in her career. (Ferry Publications Library)*

continuing to Rotterdam (Westerkade) to unload her cargo. Trains, decorated with both the British and Dutch flags, duly left for Amsterdam at 07.08 and Rotterdam at 07.16. Two international trains, the 'Noord Express' and the 'Zuid Express', also left for Berlin and Basle. Later that day the *Cambridge* berthed at the Hook of Holland, on passage between Rotterdam and Harwich, to embark passengers for England.

The timings of the period showed the Continental Boat Express leaving London (Liverpool Street) at 20.00, with arrival at the Hook of Holland at 05.50 the following morning. Amsterdam could be reached at 08.26 and Berlin at 22.36.

The *Chelmsford* lasted seventeen years on the Harwich route before being sold to the Great Western Railway who used her, as the *Bretonne*, on their Plymouth-Nantes service. After one year the service was closed and the vessel was resold to Greece where she served until 1933.

In 1894, Earle's of Hull built a trio of ships which were to replace the route's final three paddle steamers, the *Princess of Wales*, *Adelaide* and *Claud Hamilton*. The new ships were the first to be given the grander names of Continental cities to which it was now possible to travel via the Hook of Holland route. Although the homely Great Eastern names were retained for the cargo steamers, the new naming policy for the passenger fleet demonstrated an outward-looking

*The **Berlin** was one of a trio of steamers built at Hull in 1894. She was lost off the Hook of Holland in 1907 in the route's worst disaster. (G E Langmuir collection)*

*The cargo steamer **Cromer** of 1902 was the first of four ships built for the Rotterdam cargo service but the only one to serve a full career on the route. (G E Langmuir collection)*

company whose horizons stretched far beyond the flat fields of East Anglia.

Each costing some £75,000 to build, the first ship of the trio – named *Berlin* – arrived early in 1894, followed by the *Amsterdam* and the *Vienna* in October. Their hulls were divided into eight watertight compartments while passenger accommodation was spaced over three decks. An entrance hall, luxury cabins, the ladies' cabin and the dining room were situated on the main deck, while extra cabins were fitted one deck below. The First Class accommodated some 218 passengers while the Second Class, situated at the stern and the after 'tween deck, accommodated an extra 120 persons. Bunker capacity was for about 150 tons of coal and the ships consumed about four tons of coal each hour. The machinery of the three new ships was similar to that of the *Chelmsford* but they were wider in the beam and carried fifty extra passengers.

At Flushing, the excellent rail connections saw the rival service to England continuing to thrive but after the opening of the Hook of Holland in 1893, the Zeeland Steamship Company began to feel the pinch of competition. The Great Eastern Railway won the contract for mail from England in 1898 but the Zeeland Steamship Company retained the Dutch mail contract which they had held since 1876. In response to the Great Eastern's three new steamers, in 1895 they had introduced three fast new paddle steamers onto their Queenborough link, but by and large the rivals existed without ever seriously endangering the existence of each other.

THE BERLIN DISASTER

The most tragic incident that the Harwich-Hook of Holland service has ever experienced sadly befell the *Berlin*. Half-an-hour off the Hook of Holland at about 05.15 on Thursday 21st February 1907 she was swept onto the end of the North Pier at the entrance of the New Waterway. The crossing had been quite appalling in north west storm force winds and passengers must have found the distant lights of the Hook of Holland more than usually inviting.

Following her stranding, the poor *Berlin* was lashed by the full force of the sea and it was not long before she began to break up and her forward part sank. The grounding was sighted from the signal station at the Hook of Holland (on the site of the present radar station) and the lifeboat was immediately sent out to assist. Although she managed to reach the stricken *Berlin* at about 06.30, conditions were so bad that she was unable to approach, and mechanical problems later forced her back into the safety of the harbour. As the cold and cascading seas continued to break upon the remains of the steamer, so more and more wet and frightened passengers were swept away. Although 128 were lost, 15 people amazingly survived when on the following day they were able to be rescued from the pier itself.

The cargo steamer *Clacton* had left Harwich shortly after the *Berlin* had sailed and encountered her wreck at 08.00. Such were the sea conditions that the *Clacton*'s Captain could not assist through fear of his own ship being swept onto the mole.

The *Berlin*'s Master, Captain Precious, was blamed for the disaster. He had been advised not to sail but it was typical of him that he did. It remains the worst ever disaster in the history of the service.

At the end of 1990, two steam boilers from the *Berlin* were salvaged during dredging works near the North Pier. One of the fire-doors and some pieces of coal found in the furnace are presently on display in the local Lifeboat Museum in the Hook of Holland.

The other two 1894 sisters were also involved in groundings. On 22nd August 1906, the *Amsterdam* had run onto the North Pier at the Hook of Holland during dense fog. She was refloated the next day with the aid of several tugs and the cargo steamer *Clacton* which, after helping to free the stranded passenger ship, promptly ran aground herself!

The *Vienna* was in trouble on 18th January 1908 when she ran aground on the Maasvlakte during dense fog while five days later, again in thick fog, the *Amsterdam* collided with the anchored American ship *Axminster*. The collision occurred near the Maas lightship which was located off the entrance to the New Waterway. The *Amsterdam* started taking in water and so passengers were transferred to the *Axminster* and then to a pilot vessel which landed them at the Hook of Holland. The passenger steamer was dry-docked in Rotterdam after discharging her cargo at the Hook of Holland and the *Vienna* crossed light from Harwich to relieve her.

All the Great Eastern's ships at one time or another served the Harwich-Antwerp link and on 19th January 1911 the *Vienna* was in collision with the Blue Funnel Line's *Patroclus* in the River Schelde. Although her stern was badly damaged, she managed to return to Harwich.

Earle's last passenger vessel for the Great Eastern

Railway was the *Dresden* of 1897. She was launched in November and boasted a higher bridge than the previous ships. She has gone down in history as the ship in which the world-famous German marine engineer Dr. Rudolph Diesel was travelling in October 1913 when he mysteriously disappeared and was assumed lost overboard.

Until now, the Antwerp service had mainly received its tonnage as second-hand vessels no longer required on the Hook of Holland crossing, but in March 1902 a vessel was launched by Gourlay of Dundee which was to change this policy. The vessel was built on Tayside as at that time Earle's of Hull had a full order book and she was to be the Harwich fleet's last reciprocating steamer. This was the famous *Brussels* which from time to time did operate to the Hook of Holland on relief sailings and which during the Great War captured the imagination of the British public.

The year 1902 also saw Gourlay deliver the 812 gross ton cargo steamer *Cromer*, ample evidence of the decreasing space for freight on the passenger service which was, by this time, breaking all records. So successful was the *Cromer* that the *Yarmouth* followed in 1903, while Earle's delivered the *Clacton* and the *Newmarket* in 1904 and 1907.

The *Yarmouth* was the route's mystery ship. On 27th October 1908 she left the Hook of Holland under the command of Captain Avis at 10.30 with 430 tons of cargo (including 192 tons of meat), three furniture vans on deck and one passenger who could not have enjoyed the rather spartan atmosphere experienced on board.

The *Yarmouth* was later seen passing the Outer Gabbard light vessel listing badly but not enough for her Master to call for assistance. Just what happened is not known – suffice to say that the ship was never seen again. After she failed to

*The ill-fated **Berlin** was wrecked on the North Pier of the New Waterway, after stranding herself in the early hours of 21st February 1907. (Ferry Publications Library)*

*Seen here fitting-out at Clydebank is the third of the Great Eastern's turbine steamers the **St. Petersburg**. (Ferry Publications Library)*

arrive at Harwich, the *Vienna* was sent to look for her and HMS. *Blake* also took up the search. Close to the Outer Gabbard light they discovered some wreckage and lifebelts together with a single body.

At the Hook of Holland in 1903 the new America Wharf was opened on the site of the present Stena Line passenger terminal. It was constructed by using iron screw piles and wooden decking and was used by the trans-Atlantic liners of the Holland America Line. In those days the depth of water at Rotterdam was not sufficient for them to berth at all states of the tide and so passengers would be disembarked at the Hook of Holland and the ships would sail up river on the tide to discharge cargo. When, after the First World War, the river was deepened, the liner traffic ceased calling at the Hook of Holland. In August 1932 a stevedore company called 'New Fruit Wharf' took over the wharf and its large warehouse and by 1933 the Hook of Holland was Europe's largest importer of fruit. Trains of up to forty wagons regularly left the station for various Continental destinations and this continued until the outbreak of war in 1939.

After the war the now-named 'Fruit Wharf' was used by the troopships and the shed became a NAAFI facility. A fire on 1st November 1956 destroyed both the decking and the former warehouse but these were replaced. It was not until 1980 that the 'Fruit Wharf' was demolished, although the present Stena Line berth stands on this same site.

CONTINUED PROGRESS

During 1904 the Harwich-Hook of Holland service was modified by removing the call at Rotterdam and in consequence of this both the *Norwich* and the *Ipswich* were sold. Although Rotterdam still remained as the terminal of the cargo ship service, this was terminated in 1968 when it was replaced by a joint British Rail/SMZ container service. This was closed in 1973.

The freight ships continued to use the Parkkade until 1933 when they moved to a new terminal in Merwehaven. As this was destroyed in the war a temporary berth was used in Lekhaven until the pre-war terminal was reopened in 1950. The short-lived container service was based at the Europe Container Terminal in Margriethaven.

In June 1903 the South Eastern & Chatham Railway had introduced the world's first turbine-driven cross-Channel steamer onto the Dover-Calais route. Other railway companies soon followed and the Great Eastern were not slow to see the advantages of this superior form of propulsion.

The expertise was on the River Clyde in Scotland, and the East Coast yards to which the Great Eastern Railway had remained loyal for so long were never again asked to build major passenger units for the North Sea link.

The yard in which Harwich now placed their faith and future for over fifty years was John Brown's at Clydebank, a

*The cargo vessel **Felixstowe** joined the Rotterdam cargo link in 1918 and is seen here at the end of her career at Weymouth in 1948. Between 1942-46 she was renamed **Colchester**. (Ferry Publications Library)*

*Purchased in 1917 to replace war losses, the **Kilkenny** served for ten more years in a cargo capacity, trading as the **Frinton**. (Ferry Publications Library)*

name better known perhaps for being responsible for the construction of the mighty Cunarders *Queen Mary*, *Queen Elizabeth* and *Queen Elizabeth 2* in addition to the pride of the Royal Navy HMS. *Hood* and the Royal Yacht *Britannia* (whose hull was based upon the plans for the post-war Harwich steamer *Arnhem*).

The Great Eastern's first turbine steamers were all ordered separately and named the *Copenhagen*, *Munich* and *St. Petersburg*. They went down the ways into the Clyde in October 1906, August 1907 and April 1910 and were the first ships for the service with triple screws.

On their entry into service in January 1907, June 1908 and July 1910, the old *Chelmsford* and *Cambridge* were withdrawn and before the First World War a fourth ship was ordered.

This is the ship that never was, for while under construction at Clydebank in February 1917 she was taken over by the Royal Navy. She was built with geared turbines

(single reduction) against the direct drive turbines of the earlier ships. Although launched with her intended name of *Stockholm*, four months later at the end of August, her name was changed to *Pegasus* and she was converted for use as an aircraft carrier until her demise in 1931.

With Parkeston Quay now attracting more traffic than it could comfortably handle, work had previously started in November 1906 on building a western extension of over 300 metres which was finally opened in 1910.

THE GREAT EASTERN AT WAR

War was declared with the Kaiser's Germany on 4th August 1914, the German Ambassador and his staff returning home via the Hook of Holland in the *St. Petersburg*. On the return voyage, the British Ambassador in Berlin sailed for Harwich. Parkeston Quay was immediately taken over by the Admiralty and the Hook of Holland service was transferred to Tilbury on the River Thames. Although the

*The **Brussels** grounded off Harwich in 1907. (G. R. van Veldhoven collection)*

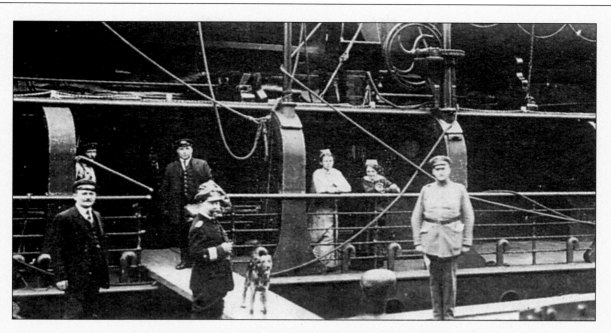

*Top: Captain Fryatt (left) and the **Brussels** taken prisoner by the Germans in 1916.*
(Henk van der Lugt collection)

*Above: This view shows the launch of the **Stockholm**. She was never to see service on the route for which she was built.*
(Glasgow University Archives)

*Right: The **Dewsbury** was built in 1910 for the Grimsby - Hamburg service of the Great Central Railway. Later passing to the LNER, she closed the Harwich - Antwerp service in 1959.*
(Ferry Publications Library)

*The aircraft carrier HMS **Pegasus** was originally intended to be the Harwich steamer, **Stockholm**. (Ferry Publications Library)*

service was terminated on the invasion of Belgium, it was reinstated after Dutch neutrality had been guaranteed. The Antwerp link closed on 9th October 1914.

However, it was a dangerous time for the ships which remained. Not only were the channels no longer marked or lit but mines were numerous, and there was always the possibility of being intercepted by units of the Imperial German Navy.

On 11th December 1914 the *Colchester* was ordered to stop by a German submarine which had surfaced alongside when, about 20 miles off the New Waterway. Captain Lawrence duly ordered 'Full Ahead' and his ship outran the raider. He was later awarded a gold watch by his employers and stated that he had previously been involved in six similar escapes from the enemy.

With most of the fleet requisitioned, the Great Eastern were forced to charter the Great Central Railway's cargo/passenger steamers *Wrexham* (built 1902), *Staveley* (built 1891) and her sister ship *Notts* (built as the *Nottingham* in 1891).

Of all the Great Eastern ships it was the *Brussels* with which the public most identified. At the outbreak of war she had not been requisitioned but was retained on service from Tilbury to the Hook of Holland under the command of Captain Charles Fryatt.

There were a number of occasions when enemy units had been sighted but, as with the *Colchester*, only her superior

speed had enabled her to escape. However, on 28th March 1915 the submarine U-33 intercepted the *Brussels* and ordered Captain Fryatt to stop.

His response was to order the crew to the after part of the ship and to attempt to ram the U-boat. It was claimed that the steamer actually clipped its conning tower as it dived. For his courageous and plucky action, Fryatt became a national hero but he was also a marked man and it was certain that every German unit in the North Sea would in future keep a special look-out for the *Brussels*. With this in mind, Fryatt was offered another command but this he refused.

Eventually the Germans did catch up with him and on 23rd June 1916 four destroyers escorted the *Brussels* into Zeebrugge harbour. There her crew were interned while Fryatt was arrested, tried and later shot.

The ship was renamed *Brugge* and was used as a depot ship for German flying boats until she was scuttled at the entrance of the harbour in October 1917. Two years later she was raised and sold, the proceeds of her sale going to charity and being donated towards the building of the Fryatt Memorial Hospital at Harwich.

The *Brussels* was towed to Leith where she was rebuilt and for the remainder of her career she carried cattle on the Liverpool to Dublin route, after 1923 gaining the prefix 'Lady'.

The fate of the Great Eastern Railway fleet is briefly outlined here:

Ship	Year	Fate
Colchester	1889	Captured by Germans 9/1916. Lost in Baltic 3/1918.
Amsterdam	1894	Returned to service.
Vienna	1894	Renamed HMS. *Antwerp* during the war. Returned to service.
Dresden	1897	Renamed *Louvain* 10/1915 but sunk in Eastern Mediterranean 1/1918.
Brussels	1902	Captured 6/1916. Scuttled Zeeebruge 10/1917.
Cromer	1902	Returned to service.
Clacton	1906	Lost Levant 10/1917.
Newmarket	1907	Lost Dardanelles 7/1916.
Copenhagen	1907	Hospital ship – torpedoed and sunk off Belgian coast 3/1917.
Munich	1908	Renamed *St. Denis* 1916. Returned to service.
St. Petersburg	1910	Returned to service.

Thus, of the eleven ships with which the Great Eastern started the Great War, just five were returned to them for future use. Fortunately the Great Central Railway were again able to assist and a number of their steamers were chartered for use on the Harwich routes, two of which – the *Accrington* and *Dewsbury* – were to reappear after the Second World War.

The Harwich ships which carried the names of German cities were renamed during the war and the *Dresden* and *Munich* became the friendlier *Louvain* and *St. Denis*. Now, with political changes taking place in revolutionary Russia, in 1919 the *St. Petersburg* was renamed *Archangel*.

POST-WAR REVIVAL

Replacements were badly needed for the war losses and in 1917 the Great Eastern purchased the fourteen-year-old passenger and cargo vessel *Kilkenny* from the City of Dublin Steam Packet Company. Before her delivery in 1919 she ran aground on the Irish coast and suffered considerable damage.

Renamed *Frinton* in 1919, she was mainly associated with the Antwerp service which she reopened with the *Vienna* in February that year. The 'new' ship remained for another ten years before being sold for yet further use on the ferry service linking Brindisi (Italy) and Piraeus (Greece).

*Built for the Great Eastern's Harwich-Antwerp route, the **Antwerp** was a further product of John Brown's Clydebank yard in 1920. (G.E. Langmuir collection)*

The cargo vessel *Felixstowe* (delivered from Hawthorn of Leith in 1919) reopened the Rotterdam cargo service with the *Cromer* early in that year.

The second post-war acquisition was the turbine steamer *St. George*. Built at Birkenhead by Cammell Laird Ltd. in 1906 for the Great Western Railway's new Fishguard-Rosslare route, she was sold to the Canadian Pacific Railway in May 1913.

Returned to Britain for use as a hospital ship during the war, the *St. George* was purchased by the Great Eastern in June 1919 to replace the *Copenhagen*. Some £130,000 was spent on converting her for her new role and at 22.5 knots she became the Great Eastern's fastest ship.

The Hook of Holland service reopened in November 1919 using the old *Amsterdam* of 1894 and the *Archangel* (ex *St. Petersburg*) but when the *St. Denis* took up station the former ship was demoted to the Antwerp link.

On entering service the *St. George* joined the renamed turbine steamer twins and a daily service to the Hook of Holland was finally resumed in April 1920.

On 5th July 1921 the Great Eastern commenced a new, summer, service to Zeebrugge. It was operated three times a week and it was hoped that it would encourage Continental holidays which had become very popular since the end of the First World War.

Transferred to the route was the old *Vienna* (of 1894) which was now given the more appropriate Belgian name of *Roulers*.

New tonnage for the Antwerp link had arrived in the form of the sisters *Antwerp* and *Bruges* from John Brown's Clydebank yard in 1920. With passenger accommodation for 1,250 and cruiser sterns, they were followed by the *Malines* from Armstrong, Whitworth of Wallsend-on-Tyne. She

commenced service in March 1921, being the last ship to be built for the Great Eastern and relegating the *Amsterdam* to reserve. With the new vessels now in service, the *Roulers* (ex *Vienna*) and the *Frinton* were displaced from the Antwerp service.

THE LONDON & NORTH EASTERN RAILWAY AND SMZ

On 1st January 1923 came the grouping of the numerous British railway companies which brought about the creation of the 'Big Four'. The 61 years of the Great Eastern Railway came to an end and the Harwich fleet passed into the hands of the London & North Eastern Railway Company (LNER).

In March of that year, the LNER and Belgian State Railways formed a subsidiary company known as Great Eastern Train Ferries Ltd. and in April 1924 the new Harwich-Zeebrugge train ferry service started, thereby increasing the Harwich fleet by three vessels. Unlike the passenger ships, the train ferries operated from Harwich town itself and in 1933 the LNER took full control of the operation.

The LNER's first new ship for the Harwich station was the cargo steamer *Sheringham* which took up the Rotterdam route on her completion in 1926. She was the last local ship to be built by Earle's of Hull and replaced the *Frinton* which had spent her last years on the cargo service to Rotterdam before passing to Greek owners in 1927.

The most significant change during 1927 occurred on the first day of the year when the Zeeland Steamship Company (SMZ) commenced service from Parkeston Quay to Flushing, having moved their English terminal from Folkestone. The new agreement between the former rivals

*The **St. George** alongside the Hook of Holland in July 1923. (KLM Photos)*

The **St. Petersburg** *of 1910 is seen off John Brown's yard at Clydebank. Renamed* **Archangel** *after the Great War, she ended service on the summer Harwich - Zeebrugge link before becoming a Second World War loss. (Ferry Publications Library)*

dictated that the LNER would continue to run the night service while SMZ would, in future, operate by day.

It was the veteran reciprocating-engined steamer *Oranje Nassau* that arrived 'light' from Flushing on 31st December 1926 in readiness for taking up the service on the following day, while the first inward sailing to Harwich was operated by the five-year-old *Mecklenburg*.

The third of the Dutch trio was the *Prinses Juliana*. All three ships were almost identical, the *Oranje Nassau* being the only survivor of the original trio built in 1909 by Fairfield of Govan in answer to the Great Eastern's first three turbine steamers. Her sisters were lost during the First World War and replacements with the same names, and from the same plans, had arrived in 1920 and 1922 respectively from the De Schelde yard at Flushing. They were the most beautiful-looking vessels with counter sterns, long lean lines and two handsomely-proportioned and raked funnels between pole masts of identical rake.

Both the LNER Harwich-Hook of Holland route and the SMZ link between Harwich and Flushing boasted excellent railway connections with Germany. The former ran via Rotterdam, Utrecht and Arnhem while the latter was via the now partly defunct line linking Flushing with Bergen op Zoom, Tilburg, Uden and Beugen.

The LNER now embarked on a modernisation programme which saw the remaining 1894 twins *Amsterdam* (latterly used on the Rotterdam cargo service) and *Roulers* (ex *Vienna*) and the replacement vessel *St. George* all pass for breaking at Blyth, Northumberland, in a fifteen-month period from December 1928.

The replacements inevitably came from Clydebank in the form of three most impressive steamers, the sisters *Vienna*, *Prague* and *Amsterdam*. They were over 4,000 gross tons with a speed of 21 knots and measured 366 ft. by 50 ft..

The *Vienna* was the first on station, arriving at Parkeston Quay early in July 1929, followed by the *Prague* in February 1930 and the *Amsterdam* two months later.

The first of the trio made courtesy calls to Amsterdam (on 12-13th July) and Rotterdam (on 13th-14th July) before making her maiden voyage from Harwich on Monday 15th July 1929. This sailing was duplicated by the *St. George* which, after disembarking her passengers the following morning, sailed 'light' to England at the conclusion of her final sailing before being broken up.

The *Prague*'s maiden voyage was on 1st March, but five days later dense fog was already interfering with her schedules. The same fog saw the *Bruges* disembarking her passengers at Flushing while on her way up the River Schelde on her regular service to Antwerp.

The *St. Denis* had made her final scheduled call at the Hook of Holland on 28th February, although during the 'thirties she was occasionally used to run extra, relief sailings.

The third of the sisters, the *Amsterdam*, worked her maiden voyage on Saturday 26th April 1930. After disembarkation she proceeded to the Parkkade at Rotterdam before returning to the Hook of Holland in time to resume her schedule that night.

An outstanding trials picture of the **Bruges** which was the second of the three Belgian-named ships built during 1920 and 1921 for the Antwerp service. (Ferry Publications Library)

Harwich
Hook of Holland 1893-2020

*The **Vienna** was launched from John Brown's Clydebank yard in April 1929 as the first of a trio of steamers for the Hook of Holland service. (Ferry Publications Library)*

The year 1930 also saw the Zeebrugge summer service increased to six times weekly using the two surviving original turbine steamers, *St. Denis* (ex *Munich*) and *Archangel* (ex *St. Petersburg*). This latter vessel made her last scheduled sailing on the Harwich-Hook of Holland route on Easter Monday (21st April 1930) when she duplicated the *Vienna*'s services in both directions. She continued to make the odd visit in a relief capacity.

During November 1931 work began on Parkeston Quay's second extension, which pushed the quay some 365 metres further west. Three extra steamer berths, new sheds and a second railway station (Parkeston Quay West) were included and all was ready for opening in November 1934. The elderly cargo steamer *Cromer* passed for scrap in the same year.

One of the LNER's most ambitious schemes was entering the world of luxury cruising.

In 1932 and during each succeeding summer until the outbreak of war, the *Vienna* offered a series of Friday night to Monday morning sorties. These usually combined visits to the Dutch ports of Amsterdam and Rotterdam, or the Belgian ports of Antwerp and Zeebrugge, or proceeded up the River Seine to visit Rouen. Occasionally a 'Mystery Cruise' would be offered when passengers usually awoke to find themselves in the Channel Islands. So successful had these become that in early 1936 the LNER Marine Department at Harwich decided to extend the *Vienna*'s boat deck aft in order to increase facilities.

The SMZ vessel *Oranje Nassau* had also been involved in weekend cruising during 1929, berthing at the Hook of Holland and sailing as far afield as Cowes (Isle of Wight) and Torquay.

During the inter-war period the spare Antwerp ship regularly made extra sailings to the Hook of Holland when

*Early in 1936 the **Vienna**'s shelter deck is seen in the course of being extended in readiness for her weekend cruise programme. (Ferry Publications Library)*

traffic was heavy. In connection with the World Scout Jamboree in the Netherlands during July and August 1937, the *Prinses Juliana* and the *Oranje Nassau* also made extra sailings, as did the New Medway Steam Packet Company's excursion steamers *Queen of Thanet, Queen of Kent, Queen of the Channel* and *Royal Sovereign*.

Late in 1937 SMZ ordered a pair of new ships from De Schelde at Flushing. The new vessels were the first to be fitted with diesel propulsion and boasted accommodation for a massive 1,800 passengers. The new grey-hulled *Koningin Emma* and *Prinses Beatrix* presented a vastly different profile from that of the rest of the fleet when they arrived at Parkeston Quay for the first time in June and July 1939.

It is of interest that the SMZ fleet never contained a

*The **Prague** leaving Parkeston Quay immediately after the Second World War. (Ferry Publications Library)*

turbine steamer – the Dutch going directly from steam reciprocating engines to diesels.

BACK TO WAR

On Thursday 31st August 1939 the *Amsterdam* sailed from the Hook of Holland for the final time and after the *Prague* had followed her westwards on 1st September the service was to be closed for six years. On the following day Parkeston Quay was again requisitioned by the Admiralty and on 3rd September the United Kingdom declared war on Nazi Germany.

The first casualty of the war was the cancellation of the *Vienna*'s weekend cruise to Antwerp and Zeebrugge. The Navy moved into Parkeston Quay and renamed it HMS. *Badger*, while the LNER fleet was repainted grey, bridges were protected with sandbags and crews were trained to handle machine guns.

On the second day after the invasion of the Netherlands, while on passage between Flushing and IJmuiden with Dutch troops, SMZ lost their steamer *Prinses Juliana* of 1920. On 12th May 1940, under the command of Captain J.P. Nonhebel, the steamer was off the mouth of the Maas at about 08.40 when she was unsuccessfully attacked by enemy aircraft. A second attack took place at 10.00 when the ship was strafed by bombs and machine-gun fire. Heavy explosions near the ship caused ruptures in her hull as a result of which she took on water and developed a list. The explosions also fractured steam pipes and damaged the steering gear and she became unmanageable. At 10.20 the order was given to 'abandon ship' and with the assistance of tugs the *Prinses Juliana* was grounded north of the Hook of Holland.

The ship later broke in two and was used by the Germans as a target vessel. It was to be the only SMZ loss of the war. Her bell was salvaged and can be seen today in the Het Jagershuis restaurant next door to the Ferry Museum at the Hook of Holland.

The new motor ships *Koningin Emma* and *Prinses Beatrix* escaped to England on 10th May while the next day saw the *Oranje Nassau* and the *Mecklenburg* follow them to safety. The 1939 twins were renamed *Queen Emma* and *Princess Beatrix* by the Royal Navy, and during 1942 they took part as landing vessels for the commando raids on the Lofoten Islands in March, on Bayonne in April, on Dieppe in August and during November near Oran in North Africa.

In the following April they took their part in the famous 'Moonlight Squadron' transporting troops between Algiers and Bone. The 'Emma' landed troops on the island of Panteleria in May, while in June came the Sicily landings. On 6th June 1944 came the D-Day Landings, when the *Queen Emma* together with the *Mecklenburg* formed part of the invasion fleet in the liberation of Europe.

After the war in Europe was over, both the *Queen Emma* and the *Princess Beatrix* sailed to the Far East where they landed French troops near Saigon (Vietnam). Later they were at Penang when the Japanese surrendered, before repatriating thousands of women and children to Batavia, Semarang and Surabaya. After six years of wandering the oceans, both Dutch ships returned to Flushing undamaged and unrecognisable. It was not until 31st May 1948 that they were to return to civilian service operating the daylight link between the Hook of Holland and Harwich.

The Harwich fleet of the LNER was dealt a devastating blow by its war losses. When in May 1940 Germany attacked the Low Countries, the Antwerp steamer *Malines* and the *St. Denis* (ex *Munich* of 1908) were sent to Rotterdam to evacuate British civilians and both were caught in the port when the Germans arrived. The crew of the *St. Denis* scuttled her where she lay, while the *Malines* sailed in the dark along an unlit river and beneath enemy guns with her 2,000 passengers, including the crew of the *St. Denis*, to Tilbury.

The *Malines* made more mercy trips to evacuate troops after Belgium was overrun. Off the French coast, near Dunkirk, she saved 1,000 men from the torpedoed British

*A majestic-looking **Vienna** seen at speed during trials on the Firth of Clyde. (G E Langmuir collection)*

*The third of the **Vienna** class entered service in 1930 as the **Amsterdam**. During the war she was the last ship to leave Le Havre before being rebuilt as a hospital ship. She was mined off the French coast in August 1944. (Ferry Publications Library)*

destroyer HMS *Grafton*. During the evacuation of Dunkirk, the *Prague* made three trips until on 1st June 1940, with as many as 3,000 troops on board, she sprang a leak following enemy action, after which Captain Baxter grounded her on the English coast near Deal. The vessel was later salvaged and she was towed to London where a new stern section was fitted. She took up service operating from Aberdeen to the Shetland Islands during which time she was again damaged by German bombs. Rebuilt as a hospital ship in 1944, she was crewed by her LNER personnel and American medical staff and was used to bring wounded Americans from mainland Europe to Britain. Between June 1944 and March 1945 she made 57 trips to the Normandy Beaches.

The *Prague*'s sister ship, the *Amsterdam*, sailed from Parkeston Quay on 7th September 1939 and during the early part of the war served as a troop-ship, transporting military staff to France. Later she moved to the Aberdeen-Shetland link before, in December 1943, she was converted to a Landing Ship (Infantry) in readiness for the Normandy Landings. She was serving as a hospital ship when on 7th August 1944 she struck a mine in the English Channel and sank with a large loss of life.

At St. Valery the boats of the 1910 *Archangel* (ex *St. Petersburg*) evacuated troops from the beaches while under hostile fire. In May 1941 the same vessel was on passage between Kirkwall (Orkney) and Aberdeen when she was attacked and sunk off the Scottish coast with the loss of seventeen lives.

The Antwerp steamer *Bruges* was bombed off Le Havre where she was grounded and abandoned by her crew in June 1940. Her sister ship *Malines* was sunk on 29th July 1942 off the Egyptian coast near Port Said. The remaining vessel of the trio, the *Antwerp*, became the Royal Navy escort vessel

HMS *Antwerp* and survived the war.

The cargo ship *Felixstowe* (renamed HMS *Colchester*) became a salvage vessel and also survived to serve the route once more.

The other cargo ship *Sheringham* joined the Ministry of War Transport and was involved in the evacuation of the Channel Islands.

At the war's end, the Harwich fleet had lost five of its eight passenger steamers:

Ship	Year	Fate
St. Denis	1908	Caught in Rotterdam, abandoned and scuttled 5/1940. Salvaged by Germans, became training ship and renamed *Barbara*. Post-war accommodation ship. Scrapped 1950.
Archangel	1910	Bombed off East Scotland en route Kirkwall-Aberdeen 5/1941.
Antwerp	1920	Survived war but retained for trooping.
Bruges	1920	Bombed near Le Havre 6/1940.
Malines	1922	Sunk off Port Said 7/1942. Raised and scrapped 1948.
Vienna	1929	Survived war but retained for trooping.
Prague	1930	Returned to service.
Amsterdam	1930	Mined off Normandy Beaches 8/1944.

*A view of the **Vienna** as a troop ship alongside the Fruitwharf in Hook of Holland in the late 1950's. (Ferry Publications Library)*

*The first post-war arrival of the **Prague** at the Hook of Holland on 15th November 1945. (Henk van der Lugt collection)*

*Another view of first post-war arrival of the **Prague** at the Hook of Holland. (Henk van der Lugt collection)*

In addition, two of the three Harwich-Zeebrugge train ferries were sunk.

Thus both of the original remaining turbine steamers were lost, as were two out of the three Antwerp steamers and the final ship of the Hook of Holland trio. Of the three vessels that remained, two were retained for trooping purposes and were never to see civilian service again. This left the *Prague* as the only pre-war passenger ship available to the LNER.

With no ships with which to run the summer Zeebrugge passenger service after the war, the link was discontinued. With no vessels available to operate to Antwerp, the LNER brought in the former Great Central Railway passenger/cargo steamers *Accrington* and *Dewsbury* (built in 1910 by Earle's of Hull) which were introduced on the route in 1946 and offered passenger capacity for just 77. With two old vessels such as these, the route failed to attract its pre-war patronage, and it was no surprise when it eventually closed in February 1950. It did, however, continue on a cargo-only basis with the *Dewsbury* offering space for a dozen passengers until her withdrawal early in 1959.

POST-WAR TROOPING

The trooping service for which the *Antwerp* and the *Vienna* were retained operated from 31st July 1945 until 26th September 1961 and the authors are grateful to their friend Henk van der Lugt for providing details. It was operated by the British Ministry of War Transport and was maintained for servicemen of the British Army of the Rhine (BAOR). A number of well-known short-sea vessels were used for this purpose, most of them Irish Sea ships which one by one were released and returned to their pre-war roles. The first troopships, the *Royal Ulsterman* (of the Burns & Laird Line's

Glasgow-Belfast link) and the *Duke of York* (of the London, Midland & Scottish Railway's Heysham-Belfast service), crossed from Harwich on the night of 31st July 1945. In the early days large numbers of returning German prisoners of war and displaced persons were also carried but eventually just three ships remained: the *Vienna*, the *Empire Parkeston* (ex *Prince Henry* of the Canadian National Railway) and the *Empire Wansbeck* (the former German minelayer *Linz*).

To accommodate the British servicemen, a transit camp was built on several sites in the Hook of Holland. From there special military trains ran to various parts of West Germany, but during the 'fifties this transport gradually decreased until early in 1961 it was decided to move the troops by air. It was the *Empire Wansbeck* which arrived at the Hook of Holland on 26th September 1961, thereby closing this special service.

The following vessels were used although other ships were also operated for short periods:

Royal Ulsterman	31.07.45-16.11.45	Glasgow-Belfast
Duke of York	31.07.45-14.11.46	Heysham-Belfast
Ulster Monarch	01.08.45-16.08.45	Liverpool-Belfast
Vienna	01.08.45-01.07.60	Harwich-Hook
Duke of Rothesay	07.08.45-14.09.46	Heysham-Belfast
St. Andrew	18.08.45-24.07.46	Fishguard-Rosslare
Antwerp	19.09.45-01.05.50	Harwich-Antwerp
St. Helier	18.11.45-15.03.46	Weymouth-Channel Islands
Empire Wansbeck	17.12.45-26.09.61	German Minelayer
Manxman	16.03.46-24.02.49	Liverpool-Douglas
Empire Parkeston	04.04.47-25.09.61	Cruises in USA
Biarritz	06.09.47-08.08.48	Folkestone-Boulogne

What is not often appreciated is that the Dutch Government also briefly ran a special service from Rotterdam to Harwich and London. The London connection operated from early July 1945 until the end of March 1946, while that to Harwich lasted from January 1946 until the end of September that year. The services were used by Dutch Government staff, the military and for repatriating displaced persons. Freight was also accepted and occasionally underfed children were brought to England for medical purposes.

In Rotterdam the ships moored in the Parkhaven/St. Jobskade/St. Jobshaven which were owned by Wm. H. Muller & Co., the service's agents.

A study of the sailing schedules shows that the London service was very irregular but that to Harwich was normally twice a week (Wednesday and Friday to Harwich and Thursday and Saturday return). During busy periods crossings would be duplicated and it was not unknown for three ships to operate a single service.

The following ships were used:

Batavier II	06.07.45-28.09.46
Oranje Nassau	27.08.45-29.06.46
Mecklenburg	21.11.45-04.04.46
Prinses Beatrix	03.07.46-28.09.46

A NEW HOME FOR SMZ

On 14th November 1945 the *Prague* reopened the post-war civilian service from Harwich to the Hook of Holland which was then operated on a thrice-weekly basis (from Harwich on Monday, Wednesday and Friday evenings and from the Hook of Holland on Tuesday, Thursday and Saturday evenings). The *Prague* would lie alongside at Parkeston Quay from Sunday morning until Monday evening, when boiler cleaning and other maintenance would take place. It was not until the advent of the new *Arnhem* in May 1947 that she could be spared for overhaul.

Since its foundation in 1875, the Zeeland Steamship Company (SMZ) had operated to England from Flushing. This had originally been to the port of Queenborough, then to Folkestone and from 1st January 1927 to Harwich Parkeston Quay.

The *Mecklenburg* was expected to be released by the Royal Navy in July 1945, but in the event did not arrive in Rotterdam until November, after which she took up the Dutch Government services, as mentioned above. At their conclusion she was subject to an extensive refit to prepare her for civilian service, although just when that service would actually commence was not known. There were fears that the port of Flushing and its infrastructure were so badly damaged that the service might never return there. Not only was the port in ruins, but the all-important railway connections were severed and the Company's offices and workshops in Flushing had also been destroyed. From 1st April 1946 SMZ moved into temporary accommodation in Wm. H. Muller's offices in the St. Jobshaven at Rotterdam.

The Rotterdam cargo service recommenced during early February 1946 with the chartered vessel *Lynn Trader*. With the *Sheringham* back on station on 23rd March a regular service restarted on a twice-weekly basis (Mondays and Wednesdays from Rotterdam) from 1st April.

On 13th April 1946 the *Prinses Beatrix* returned to

SMZ's **Oranje Nassau** *departing from Vlissingen in the 1930s. When SMZ's new motor ships entered service in 1939 she was 30 years old and was likely to be sold or scrapped but the outbreak of the Second World War gave her an extra lease of life of 15 years. (Henk van der Lugt collection)*

Flushing for the first time since the war's end. During hostilities she had been completely rebuilt and another complete rebuild was necessary to return her to civilian use. The order was given to her builders, the De Schelde yard in Flushing, but it was then decided that it was possible to return the old *Oranje Nassau* to service sooner and so she was made ready while the *Prinses Beatrix* returned to trooping.

The *Oranje Nassau* had spent the years from 1941 to 1945 based at Holyhead serving as a depot and accommodation ship for the Royal Netherlands Navy, and therefore needed minimum attention. In order to commence a daily service as soon as possible, immediately she was available, on Monday 29th July 1946 she was transferred to the Hook of Holland-Harwich night service where she ran opposite the *Prague*. There was no service on Sundays. The service did not become daily until the reappearance of the *Mecklenburg* which took up the day service from Harwich on Saturday 14th June 1947. The night service became daily during the summer of 1950 and year-round from Sunday 20th May 1951.

It was not until early 1947 that SMZ finally decided that their future lay at the Hook of Holland, although the Dutch Government thought otherwise and these differences of opinion remained until 1953. During the summer seasons between 1949 and 1952 an attempt was made to re-establish a mid-week Flushing-Folkestone service using the *Mecklenburg*, but this was never successful and was sadly discontinued.

Although SMZ moved offices to the Hook of Holland in July 1947, their workshops were rebuilt at Flushing and that is where the vessels were laid-up until the end of 1978, when the SMZ passenger ship the *Koningin Wilhelmina* was sold to Greece. After this time the workshops were demolished and the historic link between shipping company and town was broken.

Urgently requiring new tonnage, the LNER wasted little time in ordering the *Arnhem* which went down the ways at John Brown's Clydeside yard in November 1946. The name was chosen out of respect for the Dutch town in and near which the British First Airborne Division had been involved in the battle of 1944.

The design of the new ship was basically pre-war,

*Two views (above and below) of SMZ's **Prinses Juliana** which entered service in 1920 and was built to the original drawings of her namesake which was lost during the First World War. On 12th May 1940 the ship was bombed by German aircraft off Hook of Holland and beached. The wreck was later used as a target by the German invaders. (Henk van der Lugt collection)*

although she was built with a single funnel and, in order to pick up the cruise market once again, she was fitted out as a one-class steamer.

Prior to entering service on 26th May 1947, the *Arnhem* made a courtesy call to Rotterdam on 23rd May where she was inspected by HRH Princess Juliana. The entry into service of the new ship supplemented the sailings of the *Prague*, which at the end of the year returned to Clydebank to receive an extensive overhaul. Disaster struck on 14th March 1948 when she was gutted by fire and later declared a constructive total loss. With her passing, six of the eight pre-war LNER Harwich fleet had been lost while the two others, the troopships *Antwerp* and *Vienna* could not be used on the services for which they were built.

Of all the British cross-Channel and North Sea short-sea fleets, it was Harwich which in two World Wars had paid the heaviest price. However, the problems which now faced the local managers were no longer the concern of the London & North Eastern Railway Company.

NATIONALISATION

On New Year's Day 1948, Mr. Attlee's Labour Government nationalised Britain's 'Big Four' railway companies and British Railways was born.

The Harwich fleet came under the wing of British Railways (Eastern Region) and the Marine Section's first job was to find a running partner for the LNER's last ship, the *Arnhem*.

Whereas the Harwich fleet had been decimated by war, the Heysham-Belfast fleet of the London, Midland & Scottish Railway had remained unscathed, and so the turbine steamer *Duke of York* (built by Harland & Wolff at Belfast in 1935) was selected to join the *Arnhem*.

This steamer had been involved with the troop service during 1945-46 but now returned to Harwich where she entered service for the Eastern Region on the last day of May 1948. She replaced the Fishguard-Rosslare steamer *St. Andrew* which had been in operation since mid-April. Other Irish Sea vessels were also to appear briefly on the link, firstly in the form of the Heysham-Belfast steamer *Duke of Argyll* which allowed both British ships to overhaul from mid-September to the end of October 1948. Sister ship *Duke of Rothesay* served in January 1949, the 'Argyll' again in May and early June and the 'Rothesay' again in late September until early November that year. The year 1950 also brought a crop of visitors, with Fishguard's modern *St. David* serving between late January and mid-February and the third of the Heysham 'Dukes', the *Duke of Lancaster*, appearing from mid-April until 20th May.

On the Dutch side, the repatriated troop-ships *Koningin Emma* and *Prinses Beatrix* were rebuilt and refurbished for civilian service in 1947 and 1948, and in the latter year, while originally retaining their port of registry as Vlissingen, they took their places on the day service from the Hook of

Holland to Harwich. The *Koningin Emma* was chartered to Wm. H. Muller & Co. from 15th June until 30th September 1948 for the Rotterdam-London (Tilbury) service while in 1949 through to September 1952 the *Oranje Nassau* was chartered during the summer months. Freight quickly reached pre-war levels although passenger traffic was slow to build.

On 19th January 1950 the new British Railways (Eastern Region) vessel *Amsterdam* was launched at John Brown's Clydebank yard. She arrived at Harwich on 29th May under the command of Captain C. Baxter. A modified version of the *Arnhem*, the new ship was the third vessel to carry the name and could accommodate 675 passengers (321 First Class). She entered service on 11th June.

With the *Amsterdam* now in service, the *Duke of York* was switched to Southampton during the peak summer season of 1950, operating from early July until late September on a twice-weekly Cherbourg service in addition to a Friday night sailing to Guernsey. On completion of this she was sent back to her builders to be converted to oil burning. At the same time her two funnels were replaced by a single elliptical uptake and her accommodation underwent a thorough modernisation. The more modern-looking 'Duke' duly returned to Harwich in May 1951 and during that summer was used on the Holyhead-Dun Laoghaire service.

The year 1951 was the last year in which the Irish Sea visitors were required to relieve, with the *Duke of Argyll* back again in the first three weeks of February and the *St. David* serving from mid-April until mid-May.

During the storms and floods of 31st January 1953 the quays at the Hook of Holland were badly damaged and for a month the day service was rerouted to Rotterdam where the vessels berthed at the St. Jobshaven.

THE FINAL TRADITIONAL PASSENGER SHIPS

In the early hours of 6th May 1953, when inward-bound from the Hook of Holland with 473 passengers and 72 crew on board, the *Duke of York* was involved in a horrendous collision with the American freight ship *Haiti Victory* near the Outer Gabbard light vessel. The train ferry *Norfolk Ferry* and the Antwerp steamer *Dewsbury* were amongst the many ships which raced to the rescue. The force of the crash completely severed the *Duke of York*'s fo'c'sle which quickly filled and sank, taking eight people with it.

Fortunately the main bulkheads held and the remaining passengers and crew were taken on board the American ship before the *Duke of York* was towed stern-first to port by the tug *Empire Race*. The 'Duke' was eventually taken to the Tyne for a further ten months, during which a new, raked bow section was added, giving her some seven feet extra length.

At the time of the collision, the *Arnhem* was in dry-dock and, without a ship, British Railways hastily chartered the *Koningin Emma* which was at the Hook of Holland preparing for a cruise. She sailed to Harwich and was able to take the night service on the same day of the accident. This continued until 18th May, at which time the *Arnhem* returned. The 44-year-old *Oranje Nassau* was also chartered during the summer period to operate extra sailings. She left lay-up at Schiedam on 17th July and operated just seven round trips, departing Harwich on Fridays and the Hook of Holland on Saturdays. During the week she remained on the

British side and made her final arrival at Harwich on the morning of 30th August 1953 (as a duplicate for the *Arnhem*) after which she proceeded directly to Schiedam for lay-up. The *Duke of York* eventually returned to service on 25th January 1954 and during her absence the Southern Region's overnight Southampton-Le Havre steamer *Normannia* was also called in to assist with ten round sailings in September-October 1953.

The veteran *Oranje Nassau* had now reached the end of her illustrious career and after a period of stand-by she was sold on 10th July 1954 for scrapping by N.V. Holland at Hendrik-Ido-Ambacht where she arrived two days later. During April she had been dry-docked to remove her propellers and propeller shafts. A magnificent model of this steamer can be seen today on Deck 9 of the *Koningin Beatrix*.

With the passenger and cargo traffic continuing to expand, SMZ now looked for a replacement for the *Mecklenburg* and in June 1956 ordered their first passenger-only vessel from the De Merwede yard in Hardinxveld. On 30th May 1959 the new, futuristic-looking ship was launched by HM Queen Juliana and christened *Koningin Wilhelmina*. She was to be the first ship specifically designed for the link to be fitted with stabilizers and a bow-thrust unit for manoeuvring at slow speeds in confined spaces.

The *Mecklenburg* was retired on 25th October 1959 and three days later she sailed to Schiedam for lay-up pending sale. On 15th May the following year this splendid vessel arrived at Ghent, Belgium for breaking.

It was now the turn of the *Duke of York* to be retired from service and in September 1961 the British Transport Commission ordered their final passenger ferry from Alexander Stephen & Sons of Linthouse, Glasgow. With half an eye on reviving the pre-war cruise market, the new £2 million ship was fitted out to give off-peak excursions. She was launched on 7th May 1963 and revived the name of the Great Eastern's first steamer – *Avalon*.

On her arrival at Parkeston Quay she was officially named by Dr. Richard Beeching, the Chairman of the British Railways Board, before making her maiden voyage to the Hook of Holland on 25th July. The *Duke of York* finally paid off on her arrival at Parkeston Quay on the morning of 20th July before ending her days operating for Chandris Lines in the Eastern Mediterranean where she traded as the *Fantasia*.

The *Avalon* gave her first cruises in April 1964 and in the following ten years visited a number of popular destinations between the North Cape and Casablanca. With the increase in accompanied car traffic, it was a surprise to many that, at this late stage, British Railways should wish to introduce a traditional vessel for the Harwich-Hook of Holland route. By the time the *Avalon* entered service the writing was on the wall for many historic passenger links with the Continent. Passenger trends were changing and shipowners had to build ships to cater for these changes. Drive-on car ferries had been in operation at Dover since 1953 and both Newhaven and Southampton introduced similar ships in 1964. The Belgian Government had operated ships specially designed for the carriage of cars since before the war, and SMZ too had devised a system at Flushing whereby cars could be driven directly into a ship's hold via the floating pontoon alongside which they berthed.

*An impressive view of part of the **Mecklenburg** showing her wonderful accommodation. (Ferry Publications Library)*

The **Mecklenburg** *at sea on 2nd March 1955. During the postwar refit a new first class lounge with large windows was built on the Promenade Deck, just ahead of the aft hold. (KLM - Ref 30838)*

As early as September 1946 the Atlantic Steam Navigation Company had illustrated the ease of using a roll-on service for commercial vehicles using a converted war-time tank landing craft. The *Empire Baltic* carried as many as 64 lorries on her service from Tilbury to Rotterdam and during the early 1950s the precursor of today's Felixstowe-Europoort link had quickly expanded.

The business of British Railways and their predecessors was the mass carriage of foot passengers and car ferries were alien to their way of thinking, especially on the longer routes. The Southern Region had come into being in 1948

with cross-Channel car ferries already established at Dover and now (with the exception of the North Channel link) British Railways were re-evaluating their Irish Sea routes.

At Harwich, the *Avalon*'s reign was to last just five years before vehicle ferries were introduced and in 1974 she was to leave the Essex port for conversion to a car ferry for the Irish Sea. Had she been built to load cars through her stern, there is little doubt that she would have graced the North Sea for rather longer than she did. The *Avalon* was certainly the last of the line, but many would argue that she should never have been built.

Top: *A fascinating view of Parkeston Quay with a line-up of five vessels in the mid-'50s showing (left to right) the* **Dewsbury**, **Konprinsesse Ingrid**, **Duke of York**, **Arnhem** *and* **Vienna**.
(Ferry Publications Library)

Above: *The* **Duke of York** *in her 1952-53 state. She was originally built for the Heysham-Belfast link. She operated her first Harwich-Hook sailing in May 1948 as the* **Prague**'s *replacement.*
(Ferry Publications Library)

Right: *In May 1953 the* **Duke of York** *lost her entire bow section in a collision with the American supply vessel* **Haiti Victory**.
(Ferry Publications Library)

The **Arnhem** pictured prior to her launch.
(Ferry Publications Library/Henk van der Lugt collection)

Above: The **Arnhem** is seen on official speed trials in the Firth of Clyde.

Top left: Her comfortable Lounge with deep settees and traditional fireplace.

Top right: The rather austere Dining Saloon was very small by today's standards as it was expected that most passengers would have eaten before they joined the ship.

Right: The 'A' Deck foyer with its potted plants and light, veneer-covered bulkheads.

(Ferry Publications Library / Henk van der Lugt collection)

The *Arnhem* was the last LNER steamer to be built and is seen here during her official trials in spring 1947. Notice her large windows which were replaced when she became a two-class vessel in 1954. *(Ferry Publications Library)*

*In summer 1939 S.M.Z. introduced their first motor ships **Koningin Emma** (pictured) and **Prinses Beatrix**. After only a few months in service the sister ships had to be laid up due to the outbreak of the Second World War. Both vessels escaped to Britain in May 1940 after which they were converted into Landing Ship Infantry. (Henk van der Lugt collection)*

*SMZ's last traditional passenger-only vessel was the **Koningin Wilhelmina**. She is seen here leaving Parkeston Quay early in her career. (Ferry Publications Library)*

*The route's third **Amsterdam** fitting out at Clydebank before entering service in May 1950. (Ferry Publications Library)*

*The **Prinses Beatrix** of 1939 under tow from Schiedam to the breakers at Antwerp on 19th December 1968. (GR van Veldhoven collection)*

*The last passenger steamer to be built for the route was the **Avalon**. She is pictured here arriving at Hook of Holland around 1965. (John Clarkson)*

*SMZ's last traditional vessel was the **Koningin Wilhelmina**. She is seen here approaching Parkeston Quay on the day service from the Hook of Holland. (Ferry Publications Library)*

A view of Parkeston Quay with the
Arnhem alongside while the
Koningin Wilhelmina leaves
on the day service.
(Ferry Publications Library)

CHAPTER TWO

The Car Ferry Era

With the ever-growing public demand for increased car space, in 1966 British Rail and the SMZ announced that the decision had been made to reorganise their services.

During May, the Chairman of British Rail announced plans to build a linkspan at Parkeston Quay, thereby enabling traffic to drive on and off the two new car ferries which would be built for the route. Similar plans were announced by SMZ for their Hook of Holland terminal.

The two car ferries – one British and one Dutch – were to be the largest vessels ever built for the route. Both were to have capacity for 200 cars which would drive on and drive off through bow and stern doors.

The British ship, later named *St. George*, was ordered from Swan Hunter on Tyneside in November 1966 and was launched on 28th February 1968. She was designed to accommodate 1,200 passengers on the revamped day service and 700 on the night sailing, with berths for 550 and reclining seats for another 100. The ship, the first British diesel-driven ferry on the route, was built with twin controllable-pitch propellers, twin stern rudders and a bow-thrust unit, thereby enabling maximum manoeuvrability in minimum spaces.

At 7,356 gross tons, the *St. George* made her maiden voyage on the night sailing of 17th July 1968, the day after the anticipated start of the new service, but all was far from well. Firstly, the ship experienced serious vibration problems at speed which were so bad that the crew had to be transferred to passenger cabins. Tests were carried out at Newcastle University and at her builders, but neither was able to solve the problem. Secondly, the new *Koningin Juliana*, after having been launched on 2nd February, was far from ready for service, and unfortunately received fire damage on 13th June during her fitting-out period at Cammell Laird's Birkenhead yard.

The *St. George* therefore started operating a night service alone, alternating with the *Avalon* while the *Amsterdam* was used to duplicate sailings as required.

As for the older units, the *Arnhem* had ended service in the spring of 1968, arriving at the Hook of Holland 'light' on 27th April flying her paying-off pennant from her mainmast before crossing that night for her final westbound trip to Harwich. In mid-August she was sold for scrap.

With the new service starting, the *Prinses Beatrix* ended her service on 6th September and four days later went to lay-up at Schiedam pending sale. Meanwhile her sister *Koningin Emma* and the newer *Koningin Wilhelmina* continued to maintain the day service.

The long-awaited *Koningin Juliana* finally arrived at the Hook of Holland for the first time on 11th October, after which she sailed up the New Waterway to Rotterdam Parkkade for an official inspection. Two days later she cruised from the Parkkade into the North Sea with SMZ personnel on board.

On 14th October the 'Juliana' arrived from Rotterdam at about noon, back at the Hook of Holland where HM

*From left to right **Arnhem**, **Avalon**, **Koningin Wilhelmina** and **Koningin Emma** at Hook of Holland on 31st August 1963. The latter is departing from the Fruitwharf for a short trip at sea, being chartered by a society. (KLM - Ref 63229)*

*The **St. George** was launched on 28th February 1968 and made her first commercial sailing on 17th July 1968. (Ferry Publications Library)*

*SMZ's **Koningin Juliana** pictured prior to her launch at Cammell Laird. (Wirral Archives)*

*The **St. George** arrives from Harwich at the Hook of Holland on the newly-opened car ferry service in July 1973. (FotoFlite)*

*The **St. George** arriving at the Hook of Holland. (Ferry Publications Library)*

*The British-registered **St. George** unloading at the Hook of Holland following her afternoon arrival from Britain. (Ferry Publications Library)*

Queen Juliana boarded the ship for another special cruise into the North Sea, following which the vessel berthed again at the Parkkade.

On 17th October the *Amsterdam* arrived at the Hook of Holland at around 06.00 on her night service, and the *Koningin Juliana* then slipped into the roster at around midnight on her maiden voyage. The passenger vessel *Koningin Emma* had previously arrived on her final day service at about 18.00, and on the following morning she sailed to Flushing for lay-up, her place on the day service being taken by the *Amsterdam*.

The pattern now established was for the two new car ferries to operate a night service while the *Amsterdam* and the *Koningin Wilhelmina* operated by day.

As for the *Avalon*, she was at that time on charter to Gulf

Oil for the opening of the new Bantry Bay oil terminal in Ireland, but on 25th October the *St. George* was sent to Immingham with further vibration problems caused by her controllable-pitch propellers. Amongst other work done to ease the problem, stiffeners were placed between frames around the ship's stern.

The *Amsterdam* was immediately switched back into the night service, and for one round sailing in her place came the British Rail (Southern Region) car ferry *Normannia* (2,219 gross tons) which happened to be on lay-by at Parkeston Quay at the time. As a passenger-only steamer, this vessel had briefly served the route in September 1953 after the *Duke of York*'s collision, but now in her converted role she had been maintaining the Dover-Boulogne link for four years with capacity for just 550 passengers and 110 cars. She was

*A view of the main car deck of the **St. George**. This deck looks comparatively smaller than that of the **Stena Britannica** pictured on page 100 (Ferry Publications Library)*

*One of the wing decks on the **St. George** used for car traffic. Note the restricted height in this view compared to the modern day ferry. (Ferry Publications Library)*

The **Koningin Juliana** *was a particularly elegant vessel and very much represented the first phase of the route's move to vehicle ferry operation before freight demanded a radical rethink of the basic design. (John Hendy)*

certainly not a success on the Harwich-Hook of Holland route, being now a one-class vessel with very limited capacity and failing to fit the linkspan at the Hook of Holland.

Cars were crane-loaded aboard (even on her boat deck), but on her way to assist on the following day came the passenger vessel *Hibernia* from the Irish Sea's Holyhead-Dun Laoghaire route. She made just two round trips before the *Avalon* came back on station.

With the errant *St. George* back on 2nd November, the new integrated service was now finally ready to commence. This it duly did on Friday 8th November with the *Amsterdam* having completed her final voyage on the previous day.

The *Koningin Wilhelmina* sailed from the Hook of Holland to Flushing on the morning that the integrated service

This view shows part of the main lounge area on board the **Koningin Juliana**. *(Wirral Archives)*

commenced for winter lay-up. From now on the British ship would sail on the day service from Harwich, returning overnight, while the Dutch ship operated opposite her.

The *Amsterdam* was sold in April 1969, for about £200,000, to Chandris Lines of Greece who had obviously been so pleased with the old *Duke of York* that they had come back for more. On 5th April 1983, as the *Fiorita*, she arrived in Kos, Turkey for use as a floating hotel. The venture was something of a financial disaster and the ship was abandoned where she lay until sinking some five years later.

The remaining steamer *Avalon* was required to cover both car ferries during their overhaul periods in 1970 after which a Baltic cruise was offered. In the same year, an autumn cruise listed Corunna, Gibraltar, Casablanca and Vigo at prices between £75 and £220.

A new passenger terminal opened at Parkeston Quay during 1971, bringing an end to Parkeston Quay West station. Since the start of the new integrated service in November 1968 only the relief sailings by the conventional ships had operated from the west quay.

CAR FERRY EXPANSION

The new car ferry service proved to be very successful and by 1970 traffic had reached sufficient levels to warrant the building of a third vessel for the route. The contract for the new and larger ship was given to Cammell Laird at Birkenhead.

After a number of delays the new *St. Edmund* (8,987 gross tons) was launched on 13th November 1973. Further delays during her fitting-out meant that the ship did not arrive at Parkeston Quay until Christmas Eve 1974 and she entered service on 19th January 1975.

The *St. Edmund* was a vast improvement on the *St. George*

*The **Avalon** at Parkeston Quay with the awnings up (aft) indicating that she is about to sail on a cruise. (FotoFlite)*

and boasted accommodation for as many as 1,400 day passengers, 1,000 night passengers and 300 cars. With a service speed of 21 knots, the *St. Edmund* could, if required, make three sailings in a 24-hour period. On her entry into service the new ship took over the main sailings while the *St. George* was used as back-up at peak periods.

In 1975 the *St. George* also commenced an additional sailing from June through to September, leaving the Hook of Holland at 14.00. On her arrival at Harwich she would then make a quick turn-round to support the *Koningin Juliana*'s night sailing to Holland. The passenger vessel *Koningin Wilhelmina* also started a new day service on which she carried a limited number of crane-loaded cars on the 09.30 sailing to the Hook of Holland.

With the arrival of the *St. Edmund*, the services of the eleven-year-old *Avalon* were no longer required and on 29th December 1974 she sailed to the Tyne for conversion to a stern-loading car ferry for the Fishguard-Rosslare route. The passenger cabins were all stripped out to make way for her new vehicle deck. She remained in service until 1981 before sailing to Gadani Beach, Pakistan for breaking.

During 1975 there were celebrations on both sides of the North Sea to mark the centenary of the SMZ. Although for most of that period the Company had not served either the Hook of Holland or Harwich, their role in providing a safe and reliable seaway between Holland and England did not pass unnoticed, and the SMZ's historic links between the two countries helped to bring their peoples closer together.

*An impressive view of the **Avalon** seen here in October 1968 on charter to Gulf Oil for the official opening of the Bantry Bay terminal in Ireland. Although dwarfed by the **Universe Ireland**, the **Avalon** was at the time British Rail's largest vessel. (Ferry Publications Library)*

*The **Colchester** and sister **Isle of Ely** were built as conventional cargo vessels for the Harwich-Rotterdam/Antwerp cargo services. The **Colchester** was converted into a container vessel in 1968 after which she operated on the Harwich – Rotterdam container service together with the **Domburg** which was chartered by SMZ. (Ferry Publications Library)*

*This view shows the **St. Edmund** in the early stages of her construction at Cammell Laird. (Wirral Archives)*

*The **St. Edmund** goes down the slipway at Cammell Laird at her launch on 14th November 1973. (Wirral Archives)*

*The **Prinses Beatrix** is pictured here being manoeuvred at the builder's yard during her fitting-out. (Ferry Publications Library)*

The year 1975 certainly marked a milestone in Anglo-Dutch relations.

Two years later, further expansion saw SMZ order a fourth car ferry for the route. The order was placed at the Dutch shipyard of Verolme Scheepswerf, Heusden, and on completion the new ship would replace the final traditional passenger vessel *Koningin Wilhelmina*. She was built with passenger capacity for as many as 1,500 in two classes. On the night sailings the number of passengers would be limited to 1,024, of which 576 could be accommodated in cabins and 448 in reclining seats. All First Class cabins in the new ship were to be equipped with shower and toilet facilities, while the car deck would have capacity for 320 cars or 44 trailers and 12 cars or a combination of both.

SMZ's *Prinses Beatrix* was launched on 14th January 1978 by HRH Princess Beatrix. It is of interest that the pre-war ship *Koningin Emma* was launched on the same day exactly 39 years earlier. The new vessel was designed by Knud E. Hansen of Copenhagen and was built to combine the requirements of the route without losing the splendid traditions of the Dutch company. She was powered by four Stork-Werkspoor diesel engines with a total capacity of 22,000 hp, producing a service speed of 21 knots.

The *Prinses Beatrix* (9,238 gross tons) undertook her trials in Norway under the command of her senior Master, Captain Klaas Kikkert, prior to entering service on 24th June 1978. The new Dutch ferry was the route's largest at that time and took over the *Koningin Juliana*'s timetable while she, in turn, took that of the old *Koningin Wilhelmina*. The last passenger-only ship was withdrawn on 28th June 1978 and, after lay-up at Flushing, passed to the Greek Ventouris Group at the end of the same year. Originally named *Captain Constantinos*, she was named *Panagia Tinoy* in 1981 and continues in service today.

The new *Prinses Beatrix* took part in the Queen's Coronation celebrations in 1980, following the inauguration of Queen Beatrix of the Netherlands. Some 600 guests boarded the ship at Amsterdam to watch a firework display to celebrate the Royal event.

THE ST. EDMUND GOES TO WAR

In Spring 1982 the Harwich-Hook of Holland route was severely stretched when the *St. Edmund* was requisitioned by the Ministry of Defence for the Falklands War. The DFDS Seaways ferry *Prinz Oberon* was fortunately spare following the closure of the Harwich-Bremerhaven link, and she was now chartered by SMZ, arriving for the first time at the Hook of Holland on 11th February 1983 to cover the overhaul period of the *Prinses Beatrix*. Sealink UK Ltd. then continued the charter from 12th March until 9th June. Few people could guess that the seven-year-old *St. Edmund* would never sail again on the route for which she was built.

The *St. Edmund* was refitted at Plymouth Devonport where she was made ready for war. During this time her mainmast was removed and a helicopter deck was fitted in its place, the main lounges became dormitories and a hospital while the duty-free shops became stores and a library.

After an intensive eight-day conversion, the ferry sailed for the war zone on 18th May 1982, but the day before she arrived in the Falklands the occupying Argentine forces had surrendered. The Sealink vessel was therefore involved in transporting some 1,500 defeated troops back to Argentina, bringing about a whole new meaning to the slogan then in

*This classic view shows the **St. Edmund** on passage to the Hook of Holland in her first year of service. (FotoFlite)*

*The **St. Edmund** heads down the Stour past Harwich in July 1978. (John Hendy)*

use back home, "Sealink will set you free". Following this work, she maintained a dual role as a ferry to and from the Falklands and Ascension Island and as an accommodation ship in Port Stanley Harbour where she earned the nickname of the Stanley Hilton!

On the *St. Edmund*'s return to England, she was sold by Sealink to the Ministry of Defence and was renamed *Keren* for further work in the South Atlantic. In 1985 the former Sealink vessel was sold to the Cenargo Group and was renamed *Scirocco* for use on a variety of services in the Mediterranean. Then in early 1989, renamed *Rozel*, she started a charter to British Channel Island Ferries on the link between Poole and Guernsey/Jersey. This finished in January 1992, after which she was again found work in the Mediterranean.

'THE BIG ONE'

Following the outbreak of the Falklands War, Sealink announced that they had chartered the *Prinsessan Birgitta* from Stena Line of Gothenburg in Sweden in order to replace both the *St. Edmund* and the *St. George*. She was built

as Yard Number 909 for Sessan Line for their link between Sweden and Denmark. During construction, Sessan Line was purchased by its rivals Stena Line and all work had ceased. It had been planned to name the ship *Drottning Silvia* (after Queen Silvia of Sweden) but this did not meet with official approval and so on 7th June she was named *Prinsessan Birgitta*.

The ship spent the summer on the Fredrikshavn service with her sister the *Kronprinsessan Victoria* which had entered service in 1981. At the end of her first season, the 'Birgitta' was sent back to her builders where, in readiness for the British charter, her passenger accommodation was increased from 616 berths to 1,100.

The ship was named *St. Nicholas* following a competition run by the BBC children's programme 'Get Set'. The name chosen for the ship was particularly apt as St. Nicholas is the 'Santa Claus' of the Netherlands and the parish church in Harwich is also named after the saint. The *St. Nicholas* made her maiden voyage with Sealink on 10th June 1983 and allowed the chartered *Prinz Oberon* to return to her owners. In view of the pending privatisation of Sealink UK Ltd., the

*The **Koningin Juliana** was the first SMZ car ferry and entered service in November 1968 as the Dutch half of the new integrated service. (FotoFlite)*

*Following the outbreak of the Falklands War, the **Prinz Oberon** was chartered to cover for the **St. Edmund**. (Bernard McCall)*

*An impressive view of the **Prinses Beatrix** heading out of the New Waterway on sea trials. (Ferry Publications Library)*

Swedish ship retained her red funnel and white hull colours but the name 'Sealink' was added to her hull.

The *St. Nicholas* differed from the previous 'Saints' on the route as her main passenger areas were open-plan and she was built as a one-class ship. However, in an effort to retain the two-class system, a First Class lounge and restaurant were established at her after end. The central and most impressive feature of the ship was a terraced bar with seating for 500 passengers. The new 'Saint' boasted two restaurants offering both self-service style and *a la carte* meals.

On 15th June, the *St. Nicholas* was officially named by Mrs. Elizabeth Henderson, the wife of Mr. Bill Henderson, the Deputy Managing Director of Sealink UK Ltd.. In order

to maintain the service, the *Koningin Juliana* deputised for one round sailing.

Shortly before the introduction of the new ship, the chartered *Prinz Oberon* was switched for a short period to cover the *St. George*'s roster. The *St. George* had been withdrawn from service following her final sailing from the Hook of Holland on 5th June, after which she was laid-up at Parkeston Quay. On 20th September she sailed to Immingham for repairs and then to Falmouth where she was again laid-up before being sold to Ventouris Lines of Greece in 1984 and renamed *Patra Express*. She arrived at Piraeus on 1st October 1984 and entered service between Patras and Bari the following March. She was later re-engined and was

*The **Keren** (ex **St. Edmund**) on passage to the Falkland Islands in 1982 following her sale to the Ministry of Defence. (FotoFlite)*

*The **Prinses Beatrix** swings off the berth at the Hook of Holland on her morning sailing to England. Her older fleet companion the **Koningin Juliana** can be seen loading trade cars for the UK market. (Ferry Publications Library)*

*A powerful view of the **Prinses Beatrix** on passage to Harwich. (FotoFlite)*

Top: *An artist's impression of the* **Koningin Beatrix**. *(Ferry Publications Library)*

Above: *Prior to the delivery of the* **Koningin Beatrix**, *the* **Peter Wessel** *was chartered by SMZ. She was renamed the* **Zeeland** *whilst she was employed on the Dutch-UK service. (Miles Cowsill)*

Right: *The* **Norröna** *covered the Harwich-Hook of Holland service as from Tuesday 29th March until 12th April 1994. (John Bryant)*

*The **St. Nicholas** was placed on the Harwich-Hook service in 1984. This view shows her following the privatisation of the company with the Sealink British Ferries livery. (FotoFlite)*

eventually sold to Sea Escapes in March 1990, sailing to Immingham again as the *Scandinavian Sky II* for a rebuilding programme which took some five months. She finally emerged as the *Scandinavian Dawn*.

With the *St. Nicholas* claimed by Sealink to be 'The Big One' and able to do the work of two ships, SMZ began a reappraisal of their side of the operation. Growth had been so spectacular that within five years the *Prinses Beatrix* was rapidly becoming too small for the traffic on offer. As the British had done, the Dutch wished to reduce their overheads and operate one huge ship rather than two medium-sized vessels. In 1985 SMZ ordered a £40 million super-ferry to replace both the *Prinses Beatrix* and the *Koningin Juliana*.

As a temporary measure the 'Juliana' was replaced by the Larvik-Fredrikshavn Line's *Peter Wessel* (6,800 gross tons). The chartered ship was renamed *Zeeland*, had space for 1,500 passengers and entered service on 2nd April 1984, operating a joint service with the *Koningin Juliana* in place of the *Prinses Beatrix* which was away at refit.

During March 1984 the *St. Nicholas* went off for her first overhaul in the French port of Dunkirk and the *Koningin Juliana* was brought in to deputise. At the end of the month, the *St. Nicholas* sailed from Dunkirk to Dover to launch the new image and livery of Sealink UK Ltd. prior to privatisation that July. After berthing on the Eastern Arm, she sailed to Parkeston Quay with VIPs and press on board. During July Sealink UK Ltd. was purchased for £66 million by the Bermuda-based Sea Containers and their ships now traded as 'Sealink British Ferries'.

After her final departure from Harwich on 7th April 1984, the *Koningin Juliana* later proceeded to the Waalhaven in Rotterdam for lay-up. The following February she sailed to Amsterdam after having been sold for conversion to an exhibition ship to promote Dutch exports overseas. She was to have been renamed *Tromp*, but before the venture could start it encountered financial problems and the ship was sold to the Italian company Navarma who renamed her *Moby Prince* for service to Sardinia.

Her end was as sudden as it was tragic. Sailing to the island from the port of Livorno in thick fog on the night of 10th April 1991, the former SMZ vessel collided with an anchored oil tanker. The resulting fireball engulfed the ship within seconds and all but one of the 140 on board had perished.

Meanwhile, on 1st October 1985, prior to the delivery of the new Dutch ferry, the *Prinses Beatrix* was sold to Brittany Ferries who then chartered her back to SMZ until the end of April 1986. She was re-registered in the French port of Caen and flew the French flag before sailing into the English Channel where she then served as the *Duc de Normandie* on her new owners' highly successful Portsmouth-Caen link.

During March and April 1986, another Brittany Ferries ship, the *Armorique* (5,731 gross tons), was briefly used on the Hook of Holland-Harwich service following the final voyage of the *Zeeland* from Harwich on 25th March 1986. After dry-docking at Pernis, the former Norwegian ferry then sailed to join Stena Line as their *Stena Nordica*.

ENTER THE KONINGIN BEATRIX

HM Queen Beatrix of the Netherlands launched the magnificent new *Koningin Beatrix* on 9th November 1985. The twelve-decked ferry was completed on schedule by Van der Giessen-de Noord and SMZ decided that she should sport an all-white hull to match that carried by her British running partner. Instead of 'Sealink' along her hull, the

*In April 1986 two Brittany Ferries' vessels were maintaining SMZ operations following the sale of the **Prinses Beatrix** to the French company. This view shows the **Armorique** with the **Prinses Beatrix** (then under a French flag) in the North Sea on passage to Harwich. (FotoFlite)*

Koningin Beatrix had the words 'Hook-Harwich' on her starboard side, while 'Hoek-Harwich' appeared along the port side. Although the smart buff funnel with its black top, separated by red, white and blue stripes, was retained, after trials it was decided (with Royal approval) to fit large crowns on the buff portion.

Prior to the *Koningin Beatrix* entering service, a new 32-metre ramp (claimed to be Europe's largest) was constructed at the old 'Fruit Wharf' berth at the eastern end of the Harwich Quay. Terminal facilities were also improved and foot passengers were provided with covered walkways linking ship with terminal.

After initial problems encountered during berthing, the *Koningin Beatrix* finally entered service on 22nd April 1986. The new two-class vessel brought many outstanding features to the route, including a First Class 350-seater restaurant, lounge and bar on Deck 8. The Second Class areas on Decks 6 and 7 offered a bar lounge with dance floor and self-service restaurant. Up to 2,100 passengers could be accommodated, 1,296 in berths. On the vehicle decks no fewer than 485 cars could be accommodated. In the engine room, four MAN-B&W diesel engines develop an output of 19,360 kW, giving her a service speed of 21 knots.

With the two jumbo-ferries in service the *St. Nicholas* would offer a morning sailing from Harwich with an evening sailing from the Hook of Holland, while the *Koningin Beatrix* worked in the opposite direction.

During the refit period in January 1987, the DFDS Seaways ferry *Dana Anglia* was chartered to cover the services of both regular vessels, although the 24-hour refits in 1988 meant that chartering was not necessary.

FROM CROWN LINE TO STENA

SMZ was 70% state owned. A further 25% of its shares were held by Internatio Muller in Rotterdam and the remaining 5% were traded on the stockmarket. When in 1988, the Dutch Minister of Transport and Public Works announced that the Government was to sell its controlling interest, SMZ adopted an interim trade name of Crown Line. They heavily promoted the *Koningin Beatrix* cruise ferry concept with Crown Line replacing the words 'Hoek-Harwich' on her hull.

Three new visitors briefly appeared on the route during January 1989. When the *St. Nicholas* sailed to Wilton at Schiedam for annual overhaul on 8th January her schedules were taken by the former Sealink Channel Islands ferry *Earl Granville* while ro-ro traffic was transported by the chartered *Mercandian Universe*. The *St. Nicholas* returned to service on 19th January and four days later the *Koningin Beatrix* sailed to Schiedam for her own overhaul. In her place on an eleven-day charter came Brittany Ferries' newly purchased *Duchesse Anne*, fresh from a £2.4 million refit in Germany. The vessel was built for the Irish company B&I as the *Connaught* in 1979.

By early 1989 four prospective buyers, Sealink British Ferries, Nedlloyd, Johnson Line and Stena Line had entered the race to purchase SMZ. Despite a strong bid from Sealink BF it was the offer by Stena Line of 6,750 Guilders for each 250 Guilder share that was finally accepted.

The official transfer of the Dutch Government's holding in SMZ to Stena Line took place on board the *Koningin Beatrix* on 22nd June 1989, when the Minister of Transport, Mrs Smit-Kroes and the President of Stena Line, Mr. Lars-Erik Ottosson completed the necessary documentation.

SMZ was one of the oldest companies in Holland and its proud boast was that in all of its 114 years it had never lost a ship during peace time. The cost of securing the *Koningin Beatrix* and the Crown Line business was reported as being £33 million.

In August 1989 the crowns from the funnel of the *Koningin Beatrix* were removed and it was repainted in Stena Line red with the large white 'S'. On the last day of that month, the ship's new Stena Line house-flag was officially presented to Captain J. Nagel and this was raised at 10.00 on the following day when the SMZ house-flag was lowered for the final time. Thus from 1st September 1989 SMZ/Crown Line became known as Stena Line BV, a subsidiary of Stena Line AB which itself was 60% owned by the Sten A Olsson family via Stena Rederi AB. The *Koningin Beatrix* was now owned by Stena Line AB and chartered back to Stena Line BV.

Whilst taking over SMZ, Stena AB had also been trying to buy Sealink British Ferries from its parent company, Sea Containers. In March 1989 they acquired a 9% holding in Sea Containers via the New York Stock Exchange. In December 1989 the *St. Nicholas* was sold to Rederi Ab Gotland of Visby for £37 million and leased back for five years with an option for another two.

On 15th March 1990, after a lengthy and hostile takeover bid, Sea Containers finally accepted Stena AB's offer of £259 million and the official agreements were signed at 16.00 on 9th April. On 11th April the shareholders of Stena Line AB agreed to buy Sealink British Ferries from Stena AB. From 1st September 1990, the route would be entirely under the control of Stena Line; it was a year to the day since SMZ had been taken over.

On 2nd May 1990, the *Stena Seatrader* joined the route under the Dutch flag sailing with a Dutch crew. Originally built as the train ferry *Svealand* in 1973, she was extended by 34 metres in 1982 and arrived as the first ship on the route

The massive **Koningin Beatrix** *was built at the Van der Giessen yard. She was launched on 9th November 1985. (Cor Blankers)*

primarily to carry freight. Her schedule was to depart Harwich at 08.00, arrive at the Hook of Holland at 16.00 and depart just prior to the 19.00 arrival of the *St Nicholas* for an arrival time back at Harwich of 05.00. She ran five days a week with a layover at the Hook between Saturday night and Monday. The ship was a useful acquisition in that she allowed both the passenger vessels to carry more accompanied car traffic during the summer months. Her public rooms, whilst not as luxurious as the regular ferries, were all forward on Decks 8 and 7 comprising an upper lounge, restaurant and bar area plus a lower lounge and shop.

The *St Nicholas* went to Bremerhaven on 7th January 1991 for a £1.5 million refit and emerged as the *Stena Normandy*. On the 19th she sailed directly to Southampton for trials in the Empress Dock as she had been earmarked to start a new service linking Southampton and Cherbourg, hence her new name. In the meantime she returned to Harwich on 21st for a brief final spell. The end of January saw the end of any British involvement in managing the route.

This view shows the **Koningin Beatrix** *fitting out at the yard shortly after her launch. (Henk van der Lugt)*

*An outstanding view of the **Koningin Beatrix** on passage to Harwich. (FotoFlite)*

*Tiffany's a la carte restaurant on board the **Koningin Beatrix**. (Ferry Publications Library)*

STENA BRITANNICA

To replace the *Stena Normandy* came the former *Silvia Regina* which Stena Line AB had purchased three years previously and which now became the *Stena Britannica*. The ship was built in 1981 for the Stockholm-Helsinki route and arrived at the Hook of Holland directly from Stockholm at 13.00 on 17th June 1991 under the command of Captain Bill King.

Following the final sailing of the *Stena Normandy*, ex Harwich on 19th June, she sailed directly from the Hook to Southampton. Meanwhile the newer and much larger *Stena Britannica*, (25,678 gross tons and 166 metres overall) loaded at the Hook of Holland before making her first commercial sailing that same night. The ship was luxurious throughout and a more equal partner for the *Koningin Beatrix* in terms of cabins and facilities. She was the first ship to arrive as 'one class only' with the route no longer having offered First and

*The newly-built freight vessel for Stena Line, the **Stena Traveller**, was employed on the link for a short period in 1992. (FotoFlite)*

Second Class facilities since 1st January 1991. She sailed under the Swedish flag with a Swedish Master but with British First Mates and crew.

Route turnover for 1990 had been 200 million Dutch Guilders (Nlg) with 1,041,000 passengers and 69,000 units of ro-ro traffic carried. The target for 1991 was 260 million Nlg, 1,100,000 passengers and a massive jump to 85,000 units of ro-ro traffic. As Mr. Rob Waardenburg, the then MD said at the time of introducing the *Stena Britannica*: "Stena Line would not be Stena if the targets were not rather high. We are almost sure that we can reach them but we need some time, (something that is not always available in Stena Line). We have learned that the Group likes speed". It was a comment that set out the future.

In September 1991 Mr. Waardenburg left as MD and was temporarily replaced by Mr. Roland Johansson who, after a brief spell in charge, was replaced by Mr. Adriaan Vinju at the beginning of 1992.

A short-term addition to the route was the freighter *Stena Traveller* which arrived at the Hook of Holland directly from her builders in Rissa in Norway, painted completely white, on 28th February 1992. The original idea was that she should replace the route's roll on-roll off vessel *Stena Seatrader* which was earmarked for a two-month charter in the Mediterranean. However, this fell through and, after a period of inactivity, ten days later the 'Traveller' disappeared on a NATO charter. She was back again at the Hook of Holland on 1st April deputising for the 'Seatrader' which sailed for her annual overhaul. During the second weekend of April the new ship was retired to the Niehuis & Van den Berg yard where she received the full Sealink Stena Line livery following which she made one final round trip to Harwich on 13th April before joining the *Stena Normandy* on the Southampton - Cherbourg service.

*The **Koningin Beatrix** pictured inward-bound to Harwich from the Hook of Holland. (FotoFlite)*

From June 1992 the *Stena Seatrader* was providing an extra round trip per week in response to a growing freight demand. By the year end close on 88,000 units had been carried but all was not well financially.

The *Stena Britannica* had been sub-chartered by Stena Line BV until 1st May 1996 at an annual cost of £11.9 million and it was this, together with a charter fee of £2 million a year for the *Stena Seatrader* and £6 million a year costs for the *Koningin Beatrix*, that was causing the problem. Plans for a second ro-ro berth at the Hook had been postponed though a new berth had recently been built at Harwich. This was in conjunction with an earlier intention of Stena Line AB to place into service both the *Stena Jutlandica* and *Stena Germanica* and take away the existing passenger ships, particularly the *Koningin Beatrix* which was only supposed to have remained on the route until 1990.

CENTENARY

Mr. Vinju left as MD at the beginning of 1993 and was replaced by Mr. Bo Severed.

On 1st June 1993 the Harwich - Hook route marked its centenary and following their annual overhauls both the *Stena Britannica* and *Koningin Beatrix* emerged in January and February respectively displaying a special 3.5-metre diameter '100 years' logo painted on their hulls.

The *Stena Britannica* was refitted with a new 'Maxim's a la carte' restaurant whilst the *Koningin Beatrix* had, by May, a new coffee shop, a 'Globetrotter' carvery buffet and a speciality 'Rembrandt a la carte' restaurant.

Various centenary celebrations were held throughout the year in both Harwich and the Hook including exhibitions, themed cruises, special offers to residents plus prizes to travel on a mini-cruise at the 1893 price of just 20 Dfl.

For the summer season the *Stena Seatrader* began carrying car and tourist traffic. Up to 120 passengers and a maximum of 50 caravans and camper vans were now allowed on board what was formerly for lorries and their drivers only. The bar, restaurant and lounge areas were all refurbished in order to provide an attractive 'no frills' service that was cheaper than travelling on the two passenger ships.

STENA EUROPE

Towards the end of 1993 it became known that the *Stena Britannica* would not after all remain on the route until May 1996 but would be replaced in March 1994 by the *Stena Normandy* moving back from Southampton. The *Stena Britannica* was to move to the Frederikshavn-Oslo route and release the *Stena Saga* (sister ship to the *Stena Normandy*) for the Southampton-Cherbourg service. However, doing so meant repainting both ships in each other's livery and so by leaving them as they were it was the *Stena Saga* that joined the Harwich-Hook route instead, renamed as the *Stena Europe*.

The new *Stena Europe* first went to Niehuis & Van den Berg on 28th February 1994 for various alterations and modifications amongst which was the removal of a double-deck block of cabins from her observation deck between the mast and funnel. This then allowed the removal of extra ballast, in turn allowing more freight to be carried albeit at the expense of cars. New gangway doors were also installed.

The last sailing of the *Stena Britannica* was from Harwich on 3rd March 1994. Upon arriving at the Hook and discharging, she left directly for Frederikshavn in the evening of the same day. The *Stena Seatrader* did one round trip in her place prior to the *Stena Europe* arriving at the Hook late in the evening on 4th March. The *Stena Europe* then took up the run to Harwich, sailing with a Swedish Flag, Captain and Chief Engineer, arriving there the next morning, 5th March. This change of ship coincided with the time that a major

*The **Stena Britannica** arriving off the Hook of Holland on her inaugural sailing. (Ferry Publications Library)*

*The **Koningin Beatrix** and **Stena Britannica** pass each other in the New Waterway on the inaugural sailing of the 'Britannica'. (Ferry Publications Library)*

*The **Koningin Beatrix** outward bound from the Hook of Holland in Stena Line livery following the demise of Crown Line. (Ferry Publications Library)*

competitor to the route, Olau Line, had ceased sailing on the Sheerness to Flushing (Vlissingen) link. Thus there was some comment about going back to using a smaller ship especially when, during the Easter holidays, it became necessary to use the Faroese ferry, *Norrona,* to duplicate the sailings of first the *Stena Europe* and then, for a short spell afterwards, those of the *Stena Seatrader.* However, it was a cheaper option than retaining the *Stena Britannica* whose services could be better employed elsewhere.

In the middle of 1994 Mr. Severed was succeeded by Mr. Heppener.

ANOTHER FREIGHT SHIP

A second freight ship, the attractive *Rosebay* (ex *Transgermania*), joined the route on 4th July 1994 on a 12-month charter costing $5.8 million. She was repainted in Stena Line livery and sailed between Harwich and the Tor Line terminal at Prins Johan Frishohaven in Rotterdam, leaving Harwich at 23.00, arriving at the Dutch port at 09.00 and departing at 12.30 to arrive back at Harwich at 20.30. The ship could carry 150 lorry drivers and 100 freight units.

The total freight carried during 1994 reached six figures for the first time at 101,000 whilst the number of cars exceeded 200,000 for the second year running. However, the Channel Tunnel had opened that same year and was increasingly making its presence felt as regards frequency and the speed of transiting goods, even as far round as Holland where initially its effects were deemed as being minimal.

The *Rosebay*'s sailings to Rotterdam emphasised the ongoing need for a new second berth at the Hook - the old one having been sunk by a barge at the end of 1989 - and this finally arrived on board a floating pontoon on 12th June 1995. The *Rosebay*, now on extended charter, became the first ship to use the new berth on 19th June as new freight ship schedules were introduced. It was officially opened, along with additional standage areas and a new entrance to the port, on 30th June.

THE SHIP OF THE FUTURE AND 'HIP'

On 19th December 1995 came an announcement that would later transform the character of the route. From the summer of 1997, a High-Speed Sea Service (HSS) 1500 catamaran (a twin-hull aluminium car/passenger ferry) would operate as the third such vessel to sail out of the UK, the other two already in service being the *Stena Voyager* between Stranraer and Belfast and the *Stena Explorer* between Holyhead and Dun Laoghaire.

Crossing times would be almost halved with the new craft making two round trips per day. However, this would mean the loss of both the *Koningin Beatrix* and *Stena Europe* and, as a consequence, the ending of the long-established day boat and night boat services.

In the meantime the four existing ships received new Stena Line colour schemes for 1996. The *Stena Seatrader* received hers at the yard of Niehuis & Van den Berg whilst the other three were reliveried at Wilton Feijenoord in Schiedam.

On 1st April 1996 Mr. Pim de Lange succeeded Mr. Heppener as General Manager. Mr. de Lange was formerly the company's Ship & Port Management Director whose extensive marine background included having worked at the Niehuis & Van den Berg shipyard and being involved in the design of several of the company's ships including the *Koningin Beatrix.*

In preparation for the new HSS service a total of £20 million was spent in providing new high-technology berths at each port. Two dedicated state-of-the-art terminals would provide radio-controlled berthing and computerised

*These two views of the **Stena Britannica** show, above, her a la carte restaurant and, right, her modern-looking cafeteria. (Miles Cowsill)*

moorings, without ropes or mooring gangs, as the ship held herself alongside using her water-jet thrusters. In addition, major works at the Hook included extending the passenger booking hall and converting the freight and customs office building into an overnight accommodation block for the HSS crew. This was nicknamed Hotel Zeezicht or Hotel Seaview. At Harwich new passenger and motorist check-in areas were built along with a new 150-metre-long walkway to the ship.

The *Rosebay* finished her charter on 1st May 1997 and was replaced on the following day by a much larger ship, the *Stena Searider* (ex *Scandinavian Link*), initially on a one-year charter. Built in 1969 and updated and refurbished in 1995, this former Baltic freight ship entered service having been re-registered in London. Freight ship sailings were now raised

from twelve a week to fourteen.

In 1997 Stena Line AB sold Harwich Parkeston Quay to Harwich International Holdings Ltd., a company financed by the European private equity arm of the Hong Kong & Shanghai Banking Corporation (HSBC), for £72 million, a capital gain of £11 million. It was then acquired by Hutchison Port Holdings Group, a subsidiary of Hutchison Whampoa Limited, and renamed Harwich International Port or HIP. Stena Line BV would continue to contribute roughly half the port's income.

THE THINKING BEHIND THE HSS

There was a strong feeling, at Stena Line AB Board level, that the futuristic HSS would reverse the route's fortunes. Losses had been ongoing for at least the previous six years

*The **Stena Britannica** and **Stena Seatrader** pass each other off Felixstowe on the occasion of the former's first arrival in the UK. (Ferry Publications Library)*

due to ever-increasing competition from low-cost airlines and then the Channel Tunnel.

Extracts from the Company's Annual Report for 1993, when the HSS concept was first being formulated, highlighted the cost-effectiveness of operating such a vessel:

'An HSS ferry is best suited for routes where the flow of passengers, cars and freight units is relatively evenly spread throughout the 24-hour period. The capacity of an HSS (1,500 passengers, 350 cars or 50 x 16-metre trucks and 100 cars) also means that routes with an annual passenger volume of approximately 1 million are the main ones under consideration … the HSS ferries will not suffer from cancelled sailings due to weather and wind and they should manage to cater for both travel and freight customers on the routes in question without back-up from conventional ferries … Although bunkering would be much more expensive there were greater savings to be had by employing fewer engine room staff, cabin stewards and cleaning crew. An HSS would mean cutting capital costs in half and thus, whatever the protests from traditionalists, it was either the 'HSS or nothing'; nothing being the possibility of closing the service altogether'.

THE HSS STENA DISCOVERY

With an overall length of 125 metres and a beam of 40 metres, the HSS craft was described by her builders, Finnyards of Rauma in Finland, as 'a small town that can travel at 50 mph'.

A large full-width open-plan passenger deck above a similarly spacious freight deck, the first ever design suitable for carrying heavy road vehicles, rested on two outer hulls. The lowest part of the car deck was eight metres clear of the water-line. Four General Electric gas turbine engines, two in each hull and similar to those fitted in a 747 aircraft, generated 66.5 mW of power which, when directed through 4 KaMeWa water-jets, two in each hull, propelled the craft at 40 knots.

This third HSS, named *Stena Discovery*, was launched on 14th December 1996 and after fitting out left Rauma on 18th April 1997 for Stockholm where she arrived next day for two 'visitor open days'. The craft was taken over by Stena Line BV on 20th April although her first sailings were on the Stranraer to Belfast route between 26th April and 24th May. She first arrived at the Hook on 26th May and there was officially named two days later by Mrs. Annemarie Jorritsma, Dutch Minister of Transport, Public Works and Water Management. A press launch was held at Harwich on 30th May.

The vast open-plan arrangement of the public area consisted of a raised central platform flanked by seating on both sides. The forward section contained a viewing area with bars either side, astern of which were the buffet and a la carte restaurants. Amidships, aft of a centrally-located galley, were several fast food outlets, a video wall and seating areas. Furthest aft was the shop and information desk. Down either side were various arrays of tables and seating. To reflect her longer journey times some slight alterations were made from the HSS's operating on the two shorter routes which included the addition of two cinemas and sections of reclining seats plus a Business Class section situated aft between the two small outside viewing balconies. Built at a cost of £65 million, she was seen as the future of the route, what Stena Line's public relations people called a 'Seavolution', a revolution at sea.

*Guests are gathered at the HSS linkspan on the press day for the new HSS 1500 **Stena Discovery** as the **Stena Europe** makes her way to the Hook on her late morning sailing. (John Hendy)*

*The **Stena Europe** outward bound from Harwich on her morning sailing to Holland (FotoFlite)*

THE END OF AN ERA AND THE SEAVOLUTION

An early stages idea to run three round trips every 24 hours with turn-round times of just 30 minutes was very soon dropped as being wholly impractical and so it was decided to run two round trips with the ship laying over each night at the Hook. Departure times from the Hook were at 07.15 and 16.10 with return departures from Harwich at 10.50 and 19.30. Crossing times would be 3 hours 40 minutes with turn-round times of between 40 and 50 minutes.

The route's inaugural voyage of the *Stena Discovery* was the 07.15 sailing ex the Hook on 2nd June 1997 following the final crossings of both the *Stena Europe* and *Koningin Beatrix* which each made their last sailings, overnight, the previous day.

Whilst the *Stena Europe* was unloading at Harwich, the departing *Stena Seatrader* sounded her farewell. At 09.50 she left her berth to pass by the arriving *Stena Discovery*, which acknowledged her; when passing Harwich's Ha'penny Pier she sounded siren blasts to the assembled crowds watching her leave. She was then bound for the Wilton Feijenoord yard where she would be dry-docked and repainted as *Lion Europe* of Lion Ferries, registered in Gdynia, prior to operating the Sweden to Poland route between Karlskrona and Gdynia.

The *Stena Discovery* docked at Harwich at 10.05 and left at 11.10 with 1,100 passengers on board. The forecast was for rough seas with fresh to strong north east-to-east winds yet by 12.15 she was travelling at 40 knots straight into a headwind. She overtook the *Stena Europe* at 12.50 and was alongside at 16.00. Passengers sailing on either leg of this first round trip were allowed a free drink and later to receive

a commemorative certificate marking the event.

At 16.45 the *Stena Searider* arrived to tie up ahead of a laid-up *Koningin Beatrix*, followed by the *Stena Europe* at 17.15 continuing on upstream towards Rotterdam. After some teething problems with check-in and the restocking of supplies *Stena Discovery* then left, fully booked, at 17.30 to start her second round trip of the day. Fifteen minutes out from the Hook she was up to full speed and arrived back at Harwich at 20.25, leaving there at 21.30 to finally arrive back again at the Hook at 02.00. Although this was two hours behind schedule her late running was due mainly to shore-based problems rather than any with the ship, with most passengers suitably impressed with her sea keeping qualities.

The *Stena Seatrader* was switched to sail on the old *Koningin Beatrix* times whilst the *Stena Searider* sailed an earlier-timed version of the old *Stena Europe*'s schedules.

The *Koningin Beatrix* was used as a police accommodation ship between 14th and 18th June during the four-day European Union conference in Amsterdam. On 19th June she was transferred to Stena Line (UK) Ltd, re-registered in London and left to sail between Fishguard and Rosslare, her first sailing there being on 3rd July.

HSS IN TROUBLE

The early days of the *Stena Discovery* were unfortunately hampered by a series of mechanical problems, mainly to do with the water-jets, and spells of particularly bad weather that led to many sailings being cancelled. She also became known as the 'wave machine' and the subject of what became a long-running issue over high waves breaking without warning along the coastline, particularly at Felixstowe and along the adjacent Suffolk coast.

*In 1997 Stena Line introduced their revolutionary HSS craft on the Harwich-Hook of Holland service. This view shows the **Stena Discovery** at speed in her first year in service. (FotoFlite)*

In December a fortnight of repairs was needed on the craft's bulbous bows. The work was carried out overnight whilst alongside at the Hook and for this she was uniquely trimmed down at the stern using her ballast tanks with extra lorries parked aft on the trailer deck to raise her bows out of the water.

The HSS' overall novelty value helped push the 1997 passenger figures to an all-time high of 1,192,000 but then in the early morning of 4th January 1998 came a quite serious incident that shook confidence in the craft and the route.

At 01.15 in a force 9 gale, heavy seas and doing 40 knots on a late-running second return voyage to the Hook, the stern of the *Stena Discovery* was lifted up and the bow pitched forward into a freak wave that crashed over the wheelhouse and severely damaged the forward under-section of the raised superstructure between the hulls. Known as the 'beak', this area is made of a composite material of glass-fibre-reinforced polyester but her overall watertight integrity was left undamaged. The 900 passengers on board were unhurt but were all moved to the after end of the ship which continued to sail at a much reduced speed until she arrived in port at 04.00. Fifty cars on board suffered some damage as did the reputation of the route. With no back-up from conventional passenger ships available and cabins on the two freight ships full with drivers, passengers were diverted to the Dover-Calais route.

The *Stena Discovery* left the Hook on 17th January for the Wilton Feijenoord yard where the damaged bow parts were removed. After temporary repairs were made she departed for her builders in Finland, arriving there on 30th January, a little earlier than her pre-planned visit at Easter for her guarantee overhaul where permanent repairs were expected to cost £250,000.

It was not until 18th January that a replacement vessel arrived, this being the HSS *Stena Voyager* from the Stranraer-Belfast route. She took up the service on 22nd January and remained until 4th April but she too suffered from 'cancellations due to technical problems'.

Following an investigation it was found that a vacuum effect had pulled the *Stena Discovery*'s beak away as the wave subsided rather than being smashed in under its force. In order to break up such pressures a series of fin-like protrusions were fitted to the ship's forward underside that each protected a small air vent. She returned to service on 10th April.

More significantly, the British Department of Trade then reduced the maximum safe wave height of operation from four metres to three metres though at the time of the

*The **Stena Europe** departs from Parkeston Quay for the Hook of Holland. (John Hendy)*

incident the wave height was 3.5 metres.

With the *Stena Discovery* making two round trips per day, overall capacity on the route was roughly as it was when the passenger ships were in service but during 1997 freight volumes had grown by 11% and so another ship was now needed. In June 1998 the *Rosebay* returned to sail ex Harwich at 11.30 and the Hook at 22.00, ie. the old *Stena Europe*'s times. She had previously been sailing for Sally Freight on their Ramsgate-Ostend route as the *Eurocruiser* and her re-appearance supplemented the schedules of the *Stena Seatrader* and *Stena Searider* which were sailing from Harwich at 07.45 and 23.00 respectively.

MORE TROUBLES

The first twelve months of HSS operations saw only 673 of a scheduled 730 voyages completed and the second half of 1998 saw the *Stena Discovery* still suffering from the occasional disruption.

Human error at Harwich on 24th August 1998 left a flooding valve open that caused the HSS berth to sink and strand 300 cars and 1,350 passengers on board the vessel. It was not until after the berth was repaired that cars were able to disembark at 07.30 the next day. Three sailings were cancelled with passengers either being accommodated in local hotels or given £20 and told to drive to Dover.

On 27th September problems were found in the outer port side water-jet whilst the vessel was alongside at the Hook. As a result the early morning trip was cancelled as two round trips were not possible due to the lack of speed. Even the one return trip meant an arrival back at the Hook at 02.00.

On 6th October the HSS sailed to Wilton Feijenoord for a 48-hour water-jet replacement job. This was followed by an early refit at Harland & Wolff's yard in Belfast between 8th and 29th November during which all four water-jets received various modifications. The plates attaching the jets to the ship were all renewed as the old ones were found to be cracking due to excess vibration. A new radar mast inside a polyester dome was fitted above the wheelhouse which would be less affected by wind and weather, new paintwork and anti-corrosion measures were applied whilst inside, the seating capacity was increased by 100. She arrived back at the Hook on 2nd December and returned to service two days later. Again, no substitute vessel was provided during the refit period and thus passengers were again diverted via Dover-Calais.

NEW SHIPS

In response to a growing freight market, Stena Line declared on 10th June 1999 that two new ro-pax ferries would be allocated to the route by the end of 2000. The first, British-flagged and -crewed, would replace the *Stena Searider*, the second, Dutch-flagged, would replace the *Stena Seatrader*. The *Rosebay* charter would end upon the arrival of the second ship. To be built by Astilleros Espanoles (AESA) in Cadiz at a cost of £50 million each, they would be the first sister ships seen on the route since SMZ introduced the *Koningin Emma* and *Prinses Beatrix* in 1939.

At around 15.00 on 7th December 1999 a fire broke out in one of the engine rooms on board the *Stena Discovery* as she was entering the New Waterway. This was extinguished

*The **Stena Discovery** at her Parkeston Quay berth, prior to her morning sailing to Holland. (John Hendy)*

by local fire-fighters and the next trip was cancelled. A gas turbine was damaged and for several days she ran on reduced power which, together with a period of bad weather, meant some sailings running four hours late. Repairs were completed by 19th December when normal service resumed.

Apart from a normally expected cancellation rate of up to 1.5% due to wave height restrictions, the *Stena Discovery* was altogether a much improved craft throughout 1999 and helped the route carry a record 230,000 cars. The annual dry-dockings that year saw the *Rosebay* going to the ARNO yard in Dunkirk during late November and *Stena Searider* to Niehuis & Van den Berg between 1st and 19th December. The *Stena Discovery* had her annual maintenance whilst berthed alongside at the Hook between 15th and 17th January 2000 during which two water-jets were overhauled. The *Stena Seatrader* was also maintained whilst alongside at the Hook between 25th and 27th February, with her schedules being covered by the *Rosebay*.

NEW ROUTE TO KILLINGHOLME

On 2nd May 2000 came news that a new freight-only route would open between the Hook of Holland and the south Humberside port of Killingholme. An initial 10-year contract between Stena Line BV and Simon Group plc, the owners of the Killingholme Humber Sea Terminal (HST), would start in October 2000. The route would open using the *Stena Searider* and *Rosebay* once they were released by the arrival of the first of the new Harwich-Hook ro-pax vessels. The second new ship would release the *Stena Seatrader*. These older vessels were ideal with which to start any new route as, for accountancy purposes, they were practically sailing for free.

Contrary to Board level aspirations, the *Stena Discovery* never did sail the Harwich-Hook route alone 'without back-up from conventional ferries'. High loadings of heavy freight would often cause her to slow down as she sat lower in the water though in August and early September 2000 her loadings were being restricted due to problems with the gas turbines that prevented her from running at full speed. Her schedules provided more than enough capacity for both the passenger and car markets but if she carried just lorries, with no cars, her capacity for roughly 73,000 units annually was never going to be sufficient. In the first ten years under Stena Line BV the route's annual freight figures were close to having doubled to 129,000.

The Stena empire was reorganised in 2000 when Dan Sten Olsson took Stena Line AB off the Stock Exchange and privatised it within the parent company of Stena AB. This included taking Stena Line BV more 'in-house' and the move came with a promise that the Olsson family would invest in more new ships.

ARRIVAL OF NEW SHIPS

On 1st September 2000 the first of the new ro-pax ferries was handed over by AESA to her new owners, Stena RoRo. She was named *Stena Britannica* and with her sister, the *Stena Hollandica*, were number 3 and 4 of a series of Seapacer Class ro-ro/passenger ships, the first two of which had gone to Finnlines as their *Finnclipper* and *Finneagle*.

With an overall length of 188.3 metres, a beam of 28.7 metres and 30,500 gross tons, the primary function of these new ships was to cater for freight. With a total of 2,500 lane metres per ship throughout three main cargo decks, enough for 160 units, they had roughly the same capacity in total as the three freight ships they displaced. The main public areas were on Deck 7 and included a self-service restaurant, an open-plan lounge and bar, a shop, drivers' lounge and business lounge. Decks 8 and 9 together housed 192 fully-equipped passenger cabins.

The new *Stena Britannica* left Cadiz on 8th September and arrived at Harwich on 11th September for berthing trials, thereafter leaving for Rotterdam United Shipyards at Schiedam and arriving next day at 00.30. There she was fitted with a new stern ramp as the one originally built failed to fit the linkspan at the Hook. After berthing trials at the Hook on 29th September, she was officially named on 2nd

October on a wet and windy afternoon in Harwich by Mrs. Pauline Prescott, wife of the (then) UK Deputy Prime Minister.

The ship's schedules were a 22.15 night-time departure from the Hook, arriving Harwich at 03.30 when the freight unloaded and leaving the limited number of motorists carried to stay on board until 07.00. She would then depart Harwich at 09.00 to arrive back at the Hook at 16.15. Her first sailing was the 22.15 departure on 3rd October 2000.

On the arrival of the *Stena Britannica*, the *Rosebay* remained as an extra ship until 8th October before leaving the route to open the new Hook - Killingholme service on 9th October 2000, when she departed with just 20 vehicles on board. She was later joined by the *Stena Searider* and between them they sailed alternate-day departures from both ports at 19.00 with arrival time at the Hook being 08.00 and at Killingholme 06.00.

On 11th October, strong winds caused the *Stena Britannica* to hit the quayside at the Hook, damaging her port bow. She then missed a round trip as repairs were carried out alongside.

On 23rd January 2001 the *Stena Discovery* left the Hook for a refit at Harland & Wolff in Belfast but had to lay up in Portsmouth and Falmouth en route due to bad weather. She was fitted with side directional thrusters at the forward end of the hulls and two replacement water-jets and returned to service on 16th February.

The second new ship, the *Stena Hollandica*, left Cadiz on 13th February 2001 on her delivery voyage to Rotterdam, arriving there three days later. She too underwent a stern door modification and left for berthing trials, first at the Hook on 7th March and then Harwich. She returned to the

*The **Rosebay** outward bound from Harwich, pictured off Landguard Point at Felixstowe. (FotoFlite)*

The **Stena Discovery** arrives at Harwich in the morning sunshine from Holland. (John Bryant)

Hook at midday on 8th March for another wet-weather naming ceremony, this time by Ms. Tineke Netelenbos, the Netherlands Minister of Transport.

The *Stena Hollandica* was to operate the night sailings from Harwich departing at 23.15 to arrive at the Hook at 06.30 and then depart at 13.30 to arrive Harwich at 19.30. Her first trip was the afternoon sailing from the Hook on 9th March 2001. She displaced the *Stena Seatrader* which, after having been re-registered in London, then joined the Hook - Killingholme route on 14th March, in turn displacing the *Rosebay* which went off charter on the following day. The *Rosebay* was sold to Rederi Ab Engship of Finland and chartered to Botnia Link for service in the Baltic as the *Transparaden*.

CALM WATERS AHEAD

The arrival of the *Stena Britannica* and *Stena Hollandica* coincided with a belief that the long-running 'teething problems' of the *Stena Discovery* were now well and truly cured. At times she had become practically 'unworkable' but from now on, apart from the occasional bad weather cancellation, she was operating with an almost perfect degree of reliability.

Meanwhile, the new ships, both on a ten year charter, brought new levels of passenger comfort and reintroduced the day boat/ night boat service, for motorists for which the route had long been famous. The purchase of cabin accommodation remained compulsory on night sailings, optional on day sailings, with meals appropriate to the time of crossing included within the ticket price. Freight drivers noticed a vast improvement over what were often overcrowded conditions on the old freight ships. With truckers being the principal customers, it was previously

considered as unacceptable that drivers were often forced to sleep three to a cabin.

Whilst leaving the Hook on 15th March 2001, the *Stena Discovery* was back in the news again when she lost four vehicles over the stern. A Danish lorry, loaded with fish, had been parked with its handbrake off and rolled loose through one of the stern doors, taking three vans with it into the sea. The outer doors are designed only to protect against rain and spray, not to restrain vehicles that should normally be secured in some way. The HSS returned to the Hook to disembark passengers and following repairs was back in service on 16th March.

In July 2001 a new standage area was opened at the Hook. The *Stena Britannica* underwent her guarantee dry-docking at Niehuis & Van den Berg from 12th to 18th November 2001 whilst the *Stena Hollandica* had hers at the same yard, starting on 10th March 2002. The *Stena Discovery* ran a reduced service from 7th January until 28th February 2002 by making just the one round trip a day. She would lay over at Harwich each night, the crew staying in local hotels, depart at 10.40 and return from the Hook at 16.00. This was due to a seasonal lull in passenger demand but it also saved on fuel bills.

FELIXSTOWE TAKEOVER

As a consequence of a deal completed on 5th July 2002, when P&O Ferries bought out Stena Line's 40% holding in P&O Stena Line (P&OSL) for £152 million, an opportunity arose later for Stena Line BV to acquire all of P&O's North Sea interests at Felixstowe. For around £12 million they officially took over those interests at 10.00 on 31st July 2002 but only continued the service to Rotterdam Europoort from 1st August onwards. The other services, from Felixstowe to

Zeebrugge and Zeebrugge to Dover, were to be closed as part of the P&OSL deal. The acquisition effectively locked into Stena Line BV a substantial proportion of UK traffic being routed via the Benelux countries.

On 15th September 2002 sailings were transferred from Felixstowe to Harwich and the following day saw the official opening of new facilities there, including extra standage areas and a new road and entrance to the port.

Three P&O vessels, each originally a Stena-designed SeaRunner Class, were taken over. The *European Tideway* (1977), *European Freeway* (1978) and the *Pride of Flanders* (1978) were temporarily renamed as *Ideway*, *Freeway* and *Flanders* before they became the *Stena Transfer*, *Stena Partner* and *Stena Transporter*. Stena Line BV were now operating 45 return sailings a week between Harwich and Holland with roughly 280,000 units annually split equally amongst 28 services to the Hook and 17 to Europoort. Approximately two-thirds of the Rotterdam traffic consisted of unaccompanied trailers. In addition, the service from the Hook to Killingholme was now up to 52,000 units annually, in excess of estimates and in profit.

The *Stena Discovery* was dry-docked at Harland & Wolff between 6th and 23rd January 2003 and again ran a seasonal timetable of just the one round trip a day until March. The Harland & Wolff dock was the only dock capable of handling a HSS as the underneath of the ship has to rest on ten supporting piles. If she rested on her hulls she would break!

A special presentation was made following the announcement on 13th January 2003 that the Route Director, Mr. Pim de Lange, had been awarded the honour of being named Port of Rotterdam Man of the Year 2002. This was the first time a 'ferry man' had won the award and reflected his tenacity in overseeing the various routes under his control.

A FURTHER STENA BRITANNICA

Demand for driver-accompanied freight on the night boat from Holland was beginning to overwhelm the *Stena Britannica* and so another new ship was needed. With Hyundai Heavy Industries' yard at Ulsan in South Korea building two larger SeaMaster Class of ships for Stena RoRo, it was decided on 15th April 2002 that the second ship should be chartered by Stena Line BV. Each ship cost $90 million and measured 43,490 gross tons with dimensions of 211.6 metres x 29.3 metres x 6.3 metres. They boasted 3,400 lane metres of freight space configured over four decks, enough for 200 units. The first ship became the *Stena Adventurer* for the Holyhead- Dublin route while the second became another *Stena Britannica*.

This new *Stena Britannica* (with a temporary suffix II) left Ulsan on her delivery voyage on 10th January 2003, sailing via Singapore and Suez, and then suffered a few days' delay due to bad weather soon after leaving Malta. Her first berthing trials were at Harwich at 10.00 on 13th February soon after passing the outward-bound *Stena Britannica* (I) close by the beach end at Felixstowe. She left the same day at 14.15 for similar trials that night at the Hook and then on to the shipyards of Rotterdam United in Schiedam.

The new ship left the shipyard at 10.15 on 25th February 2003 to sail down the New Waterway for some last-minute sea trials and then went straight to her berth at the Hook around 18.45. She then made her maiden voyage on the 22.00 sailing almost fully loaded.

The *Stena Britannica* (I) completed her final crossing, from Harwich, also on 25th February and left her berth at the Hook for the same Rotterdam United Shipyards. On 28th February she left for Fredericia in Denmark to be fitted out for service with FinnLines who, on 11th February, had bought her for US$75.5m. From April 2003 she was sailing as *Finnfellow* between Germany and Finland.

The official naming ceremony of the new *Stena Britannica* took place at Harwich on 28th March 2003 in the care of Mrs. Margaret Darling, the wife of Mr. Alistair Darling, then UK Secretary of State for Transport. (The suffix II had been removed on 17th March). After the invited guests had toured

*The **Stena Seatrader**, **Koningin Beatrix** and **Rosebay** alongside at Hook of Holland on 26th December 1995. The **Stena Seatrader** is laying by on the site where the HSS linkspan would later be built. (Henk van der Lugt)*

*The **Stena Britannica** (Built: 2000) swings off the berth at Parkeston Quay on her morning sailing to Holland. (John Bryant)*

the ship, she later sailed light to Holland at 11.30; she was the first ferry to be registered at Harwich since the *St. George* of 1968.

Internally she was slightly different from her sister ship. The shorter Irish Sea service required a high-capacity day ferry that might regularly cater for up to 1,500 passengers at a time but the more leisurely role of the *Stena Britannica* required a passenger capacity of only 900 but with more cabin space. The 246 cabins, with up to 600 berths, were placed across the whole of Deck 9 and, instead of where there was more lounge space on the *Stena Adventurer,* at the after end of Deck 8. A further 63 crew cabins, one each plus spares, were located on Deck 10.

The main public areas were on Deck 7 comprising a Globetrotter self-service restaurant, a bar and a forward

*The **Stena Britannica** (2000) at the berth at Parkeston Quay. (FotoFlite)*

lounge, along with the information desk and shopping centre. The forward area on Deck 8 housed a Food City, a secondary catering facility, though this was rarely used. Elsewhere there was a Stena Plus lounge, a cinema and two small conference rooms.

From 7th April until the end of June 2003 the *Stena Shipper* was sailing between Harwich and Rotterdam whilst the *Stena Transporter* was away covering on the Holyhead-Dublin route. On 1st August a new three-year agreement was reached with P&O in Europoort for the handling of Stena's ships at the Rotterdam terminal.

Strong winds on 7th October blew the *Stena Discovery* onto the linkspan at the Hook causing a three-metre by one-metre gash in the ship's starboard side at car deck level. None of the 280 passengers or 47 crew was hurt but a few vehicles were damaged. Repairs, thought to cost 200,000 Euro, were carried out whilst the ship remained alongside before re-entering service on 11th October.

PROFIT AT LAST

Throughout ongoing periods of global security worries, the fall-out from 9/11, foot and mouth disease in Britain, high fuel prices, competition from low-cost airlines and a general over-capacity in the North Sea ferry market, Stena Line BV had consistently been moving towards 'being out of the red for the first time since 1995'. The lowest point was the summer of 2001 and whilst the passenger and tourist market remained a problem a profit was finally recorded by the very end of 2004.

The *Stena Discovery* sailed to Harland & Wolff in Belfast on 25th January 2005 for her first major internal refit since entering service back in 1997. The principal changes were to modernise the forward bars, the a la carte restaurant and

*The **Stena Searider** on the Immingham freight berth at the Hook of Holland as seen from the incoming **Stena Britannica**. (John Hendy)*

truck drivers' area and to rebrand the self-service restaurant as the Metropolitan Restaurant. The mid-section fast food area was refurbished by creating a Food City whilst elsewhere new seating arrangements were installed and the Plus Lounge upgraded. Further work included an extensive repainting of the hulls and a general overhaul. The craft was due back in service on 17th February but encountered a water-jet problem when leaving Belfast. This delayed her re-entry into service by 48 hours whilst she received attention at Keppel Verolme in Rozenburg.

NEW SHIPS FOR KILLINGHOLME

On 18th August 2004 Stena RoRo AB signed contracts with the Norwegian shipbuilders Fosen Mekaniske Verksteder A/S (FMV) to build two ro-ro ferries, to a new design known as the Stena Seabridger Class, for delivery in June and December 2006. On 26th August 2004 FMV agreed a sub-contract for the St Petersburg yard of Baltiysky Zavod to build the hulls which upon completion would be floated up to Norway for final fitting-out. Each ship would cost 65 million Euro. It was later stated on 15th October 2004 that both new ships would go into service on the now booming Hook of Holland-Killingholme route to replace the existing ships whose capacity constraints were restricting traffic to around 60,000 units a year. During 2005 the Killingholme contract was extended to run until 2025.

The first of the SeaBridgers left Russia for Norway on 21st December 2005, arriving some ten days later at FMV's yard at Rissa near Trondheim. There, the deck superstructure and a prefabricated forward accommodation block were lifted and fitted into position. She was named the *Stena Trader*. The ship was handed over to Stena RoRo AB on 4th August 2006 and then chartered to Stena Line BV three

days later. She arrived at the Hook on 9th August having first called in at Killingholme enroute for berthing trials. After a brief lay-up at the Damen shipyard in Schiedam she made her first commercial sailing from the Hook on 12th August on the 21.00 departure. She was officially christened by Mrs. Karla Peijs, the Dutch Minister of Transport and Public Works, in a ceremony at the Hook on 5th September, with further celebrations in Killingholme the following day.

At 25,900 gross tons, 212 metres x 26.7 metres x 6.3 metres and with 3,100 lane metres of space for 250 x 12-metre trailers over three principal freight decks, these ships increased the overall route capacity by a massive 70%. Traffic at the time was a 60/40 split in favour of unaccompanied trailers as opposed to driver-accompanied.

The ships were code-named the Optima Project and the interiors were the work of Steen Friis Design of Denmark. All the superstructure was at the forward end with Deck 7 housing the reception area, information desk, shop and a self-service restaurant that led into an open-plan bar, lounge and cinema. On Deck 8 were 100 passenger cabins whilst on Deck 9 were individual cabins for the 35 crew.

The arrival of the *Stena Trader* displaced the *Stena Seatrader* which then left the North Sea for the Irish Sea in a pre-arranged move to increase Stena Line UK's freight capacity into Dublin. Her first sailing there was from Holyhead on 9th October 2006. (She finished on that route in November 2008 and was laid up in Rotterdam. In December 2008 she was renamed *Seatrade*, chartered to the Ventouris Group and left for Greece).

THE END OF THE HSS

On 27th June 2006 came the surprise announcement that the HSS *Stena Discovery* would leave in early 2007 after Stena

Line BV had concluded that the ship was no longer financially viable. This statement was slightly offset by the news that Stena RoRo had agreed a contract for Lloyd Werft in Bremerhaven to stretch both the *Stena Britannica* and *Stena Hollandica* with the work scheduled for between January and May 2007.

The tourist market was in a decline. Passenger numbers for 2005 were a mere 738,000, way below the historical average of around one million, whilst the figures for cars, at 160,000, were the lowest for fifteen years. The one remaining bright spot was freight at 161,000 units but it was the price of gas oil fuel that finally sealed the fate of the *Stena Discovery*. This had risen from $170 to $700 per ton in just two years and with the HSS consuming 90 tons per return crossing or 180,000 litres per full day, the figures were both mind-blowing and frightening. She needed over 1,000 passengers a day just to pay the fuel bill and at full speed she used up 20,000 litres per hour or 500 litres every sea mile travelled! Sadly, there really was no alternative.

The future for this historic Gateway to the Continent would no longer emphasise speed but comfort. The *Stena Discovery*, affectionately known to lorry drivers as the 'Shuttle', would give way to the 'Slow Boats' as the route regrouped around the two ro-pax ferries.

Performance-wise, the *Stena Discovery* had been both highly reliable and technically successful for quite some time and carried around 15% of the route's freight, ie. around 25,000 units annually as well as most of the car and passenger traffic. Her loss meant devising a way of accommodating that traffic on the two existing ferries and the only way to do that was to lengthen them. Doing so would, according to Mr. Pim de Lange, enable the Company to turn the tide on the Hook - Harwich route, achieve a positive result and secure future continuity for the whole North Sea sector. The work would represent a 110 million Euro investment.

On 21st August 2006 Stena Line BV extended their agreement to continue using Harwich International Port until 2020. Confidence in the route was given a huge boost when plans for two 62, 000 gross ton Stena Superferries, due in 2010, were linked to a possible deployment there, along with a hint by Mr. de Lange that a new route, perhaps to Belgium, might start in future.

From the end of October 2006 to the beginning of December, the *Stena Discovery* made only a single round trip midweek with normal sailings Friday to Monday. The *Stena Partner* went in for dry-docking at Damen Shipyard on 23rd December 2006 and the *Stena Transfer* at Keppel Verolme Yard on 27th December. That same day the *Stena Trader* undertook berthing trials at Harwich in readiness for her covering both the *Stena Britannica* and *Stena Hollandica* as they went away for stretching.

THE HSS END AND LEGACY

The *Stena Discovery* made her final voyage, ex Harwich, on 8th January 2007 on a highly emotional day for her crew and staff. She left her berth at 10.50 loaded with 200 passengers, 40 cars and five freight units and headed towards Harwich's Ha'penny Pier, there to swing bow-in to salute the assembled well-wishers. She then headed out to sea where after seventy minutes' sailing her Captain, Obbe Visser, who was on board on her maiden voyage, announced that speed was now 43 knots and that ETA at the Hook would be 15.20, 'after the last crossing of this beautiful ship'.

The **Stena Transfer** (ex **European Tideway***) was one of three former Stena vessels taken from P&O European Ferries in 2002 when the Rotterdam freight service was moved from Felixstowe to Harwich. She is seen deputising on the Immingham service. (John Hendy)

The **Stena Britannica** *(Built: 2003) outward bound from Parkeston Quay on her morning sailing to Holland. (FotoFlite)*

No other operator took up the fast ferry concept on such a grand scale as did Stena Line AB and most regard it as 'the experiment that failed'. On the Harwich-Hook route the 'experiment' lasted nine-and-a-half years and as the 'Concorde of the Sea' she served her purpose well, making well over 10,000 crossings. Under highly favourable conditions it was possible to depart Harwich and be alongside in Holland in a shade over three hours whilst a turn-round time at Harwich was once a mere 18 minutes, but her legacy lies in having provided a long-term breathing space during which the freight operation became strong enough to finance an expansion of passenger facilities on board what would soon become the biggest ro-pax ferries ever.

The *Stena Discovery* left the Hook on 23rd January and arrived at 10.00 two days later at Harland & Wolff in Belfast. There she was laid up and never used again. She was sold in May 2009 to Albamar SA in Venezuela and on 30th September, as *HSS Discovery*, she left Belfast for a trans-Atlantic crossing via Holyhead, the Azores and Cape Verde finally to arrive in Venezuela on 26th October.

THE REBUILDS

The *Stena Britannica* was the first to leave for the Lloyd Werft yard in Bremerhaven and arrived there on 19th January 2007. By 23rd January she was inside the 286-metre-long Floating Dock III where the process of cutting her in half, amidships immediately aft of the existing accommodation block, was well under way. An additional full-width 240-tonne cabin section was then lifted into place above the forward point of the separated stern portion in order to extend the cabin accommodation aft on Decks 9 and 10. This section was then floated away and a new 28-metre, 2,000 tonne, ten-deck high prefabricated mid-section was manoeuvred into place on 27th January. By 29th January the ferry was being reassembled and by 26th February all welding work had been completed. The new section is easily seen as being between the lifeboats and the rescue launch. The ship was now 240 metres long with a freight lane metreage of 4,100 (an increase of 700 metres), enough for 230 freight units plus 170 cars. The extra length would reduce her speed by a mere 0.5 knot and for added manoeuvrability a third bow-thrust unit was also installed.

The *Stena Britannica* re-entered service with the 22.30 sailing from the Hook on 11th March, having arrived back from Bremerhaven on the previous day.

The *Stena Hollandica* arrived at the Hook on the morning of 11th March after her scheduled overnight sailing from Harwich. She then left for Bremerhaven around midday under the command of Captain Frank Haalmeijer who was making his final voyage before retirement.

Upon arrival at Lloyd Werft the next day, she was first fitted with a new full-width section immediately aft of the existing superstructure that extended the cabin accommodation on Decks 8 to 10 and contained part of the new Food City on Deck 7. Additional cabins and crew areas were installed by infilling vacant outside spaces on Deck 10, thus smoothing the ships' profile. She then went into the same Floating Dock III where she was similarly cut in half, this time aft of where the new upper deck section had only just been installed.

A record-breaking 3,500-tonne, 52-metre-long six deck high mid section had earlier been launched from the yard of SSW Schichau Seebeck in Bremerhaven on 26th January 2007. When fully afloat two additional full-width sections were then lifted on top that extended its height up to Deck 10. This

*The **Stena Britannica** (2003) is pictured here prior to her jumboisation arriving at Harwich from the Hook of Holland. (John Bryant)*

section was then floated into place on 20th March, the forward 'join' going right across the Food City near to where the counters are and the rear 'join' being forward of the existing lifeboats. The ship left the yard on 12th May for a 37-hour trip back to the Hook, undergoing sea trials along the way.

The *Stena Hollandica*'s length and lane metreage now matched that of the *Stena Britannica* and together they provided the same overall route capacity for freight as when the *Stena Discovery* was in service. The *Stena Hollandica* was now rated at 44,237 gross tons whilst the *Stena Britannica* was 55,050 gross tons.

During the absence of each vessel, the *Stena Trader* had been moved from the Hook - Killingholme route and used to keep 'business as near normal as possible'. She took over the *Stena Britannica*'s roster on 18th January 2007 and swapped for the *Stena Hollandica*'s on 11th March until the *Stena Hollandica* re-entered service on 15th May. The *Stena Transfer*

was used to replace the *Stena Trader* whilst a chartered ship, the *Amanda*, had become the third ship on the Rotterdam service on 11th January 2007.

NEW INTERIORS

This stretching project was the largest ever of its kind with work on the *Stena Hollandica* having been especially formidable. On board a lot of work was entrusted to the Swedish architectural firm of Figura, a company whose extensive experience with Stena Line interior concepts dates back to 1986.

Both ships now had a Metropolitan Buffet & Grill located at the forward end of Deck 7 with a separate Food City Buffet located on the *Stena Britannica* forward on Deck 8 and, on the *Stena Hollandica*, within the space of the new mid-section on Deck 7. The bar areas were rebranded as the Riva Bar and featured a bow-ended bar counter shaped like

*Views of the cafeteria areas in the **Stena Britannica** - bright, functional and easy to clean. (John Hendy)*

*The **Stena Trader** is seen here at the Hook of Holland loading for Killingholme on her evening service to the UK in July 2010. (Miles Cowsill)*

a motor launch complete with glass windshield. New 'open wall' design Stena Shopping centres were installed together with areas of new seating similar to those on board the *Stena Scandinavica.* A separate dining section and Truckers Club were installed on Deck 7. The passenger complement for each ship was raised to 900 with the *Stena Britannica* now having 395 cabins and the *Stena Hollandica* 398. Cabins were still compulsory on night crossings with the price inclusive of breakfast.

NEW TERMINALS

To accommodate the stretched ships significant changes were needed at both the Harwich and Hook terminals for which a combined budget of 8 million Euro was allocated. The work at Harwich involved moving the existing pontoon ramp in No.3 berth 25 metres further east plus a new dolphin fender and a high-level passenger walkway. At the Hook the existing Killingholme berth protection piles were heightened whilst passengers boarding the ships now did so via a lengthened walkway made from recycled materials from the old HSS walkway.

Meanwhile the second new ship for the Killingholme route had left Russia on 8th December 2006 for Rissa, there to undergo similar work as on her sister ship. At the end of May 2007 she was named *Stena Traveller* and handed over to Stena RoRo AB on 12th June. She entered service on 20th June following which her official inauguration, on 28th June, was undertaken by Mrs. Bianca Balkenende-Hoogendijk, wife of the Dutch Prime Minister. With a reception lunch on board the *Stena Hollandica*, the day marked the end of an investment phase in two new ships, two lengthened ships and associated port works amounting to 250 million Euro. The new Killingholme ships allowed the scheduled departure

times to be put back two hours from 19.00 to 21.00 as well as requiring the berth at the Hook to be extended by around 40 metres.

The newly-displaced *Stena Searider* was then laid-up in Damen Shipyards. She was later renamed *Claudia M*, registered in Palermo, and on 4th December 2007 she left Rotterdam bound for Naples.

In early August 2007 work began on dismantling the HSS berth at the Hook and by mid-September it was free and ready to be loaded onto the pontoon vessel *Viking Barge 2*. It was finally towed away on 1st October by the tug *Barracuda* bound for Harwich. There the other HSS linkspan was loaded on board the same pontoon on 11th October and both were then towed round to the Harland & Wolff yard in Belfast for storage.

MORE NEW SHIPS

Ever since taking over the Harwich - Rotterdam route from P&O in 2002 it had never made a profit. The only long-term solution was to replace the three old ships with two new ones and so in the autumn of 2007 a 200 million Euro order was placed with Samsung Heavy Industries in South Korea. This was for a pair of ships similar to the *Stena Trader* and *Stena Traveller* but with 30% more capacity and 30% more cabins. Delivery would be in 2011.

This was followed by news that the two new Superferries would go onto the Harwich - Hook route in 2010 increasing capacity there by 25% for passengers and 35% for freight.

From the end of December 2007 through to March 2008 the three Rotterdam ships were dry docked with the *Stena Transporter, Stena Partner* and *Stena Transfer* in turn visiting the Damen Shipyard. All were now over 30 years old, a quite remarkable record of service.

*The **Stena Trader** alongside at the Hook and loading for Harwich during her spell on the link while the **Stena Hollandica** was away for stretching in 2007. The former HSS berth is seen in the background. (John Hendy)*

At Harwich a new passenger walkway, built by TEAM of Spain, to fit the lengthened ferries was finally opened on 6th March 2008 some 9 months behind schedule during which period, foot passengers were inconveniently bussed onto and off the ships.

It was announced on 4th February 2008 that as from the 1st August Stena Line BV would control the P&O Westbank Terminal at Europoort, this being the existing Rotterdam end of the Harwich freight service. Work started in April on a 8 million Euro investment towards upgrading all the existing facilities with the long term intention of creating a second berth. Although still in operation throughout the works it was officially opened on 15th October 2008.

RECESSION AND LOSSES

2007 was an overall record year for Stena Line BV as

*The new central section of the **Stena Hollandica** (2001) being prepared to be towed into position. (Stena Line)*

regards freight carryings but an increasing economic depression was to see that growth decline during 2008, in particular as the UK went into a deep recession and the £ falling 30% against the Euro. The company managed to maintain highly respectable levels of activity throughout the year until it all but collapsed in the fourth quarter of 2008. Freight levels into the UK were then falling by 25% with even the highly successful Killingholme route suffering a downturn. The Harwich - Hook route was hard hit with only the 473,000 passengers helping to show any profits.

Ultimately the year-end total for freight on all three routes was down by only around 1% but an increasingly poor outlook led to the *Stena Transporter* being taken off the Rotterdam service on 1st March 2009. She provided cover for when the *Stena Hollandica* was dry docked at the Keppel Verolme yard in March but was later sold to Stradeblu of Italy, renamed *Strada Corsa*, and handed over on 23rd June 2009.

Despite all best efforts at countering the ongoing recession, 2009 ended with Stena Line BV making a loss, the first for five years. The number of freight units carried on the three routes of the Area North Sea in 2009 was 288,000. This was 19% down on 2008's figures and much the same as a 20% decline in the overall total for Stena Line's other Scandinavian and UK routes. These results triggered a 2010 reshuffle of ships, the implications of which were to affect Stena Line BV.

RESHUFFLE

Upon the introduction of the new Superferries the existing *Stena Hollandica* and *Stena Britannica* were due to switch to the Karlskrona - Gdynia route between Sweden and Poland. However, on 9th March 2010 it was decided

*The **Stena Hollandica** (2001) is seen here being jumboised at Lloyd Werft shipbuilders in 2007. (Stena Line)*

that they would go instead to the Gothenburg - Kiel route and in turn displace the *Stena Germanica* and *Stena Scandinavica* to the Polish service. They would respectively each take the names of the displaced vessels.

A surprise announcement then followed on 21st May stating that the *Stena Trader* and *Stena Traveller* would leave on a 5-year charter to the Canadian company, Marine Atlantic, to sail between Nova Scotia and Newfoundland. Somewhat interestingly both ships would be shortened to fit the Canadian ports.

Their replacements on the Hook - Killingholme route would be the two new builds then under construction in South Korea, the first steel plate for which had been cut at the Samsung yard on 16th September 2009. Identified as Yard Number 1807 it was for a 4,050 lane meter ro-pax for Stena North Sea Limited, and her keel was laid on 22nd March 2010 followed by the second one, for yard number 1808, some 3 months later. They were subsequently named as the *Stena Transporter* and *Stena Transit*.

The *Stena Trader* was the first to leave and was replaced by the chartered *Coraggio* from 30th September 2010 until the arrival of the *Stena Transit*, due in October 2011, whilst the *Stena Traveller* was replaced by the *Finnarrow* in December 2010 until the planned arrival of the *Stena Transporter* in February 2011.

This change of deployment meant the Harwich - Rotterdam route would now receive replacement tonnage rather than new builds - as and when the finances permitted. This enforced situation was resolved by transferring in the *Stena Carrier* and *Stena Freighter*, both displaced as a result of Stena Line having closed the route between Gothenburg and Travemunde, with the *Stena Carrier* replacing the *Stena Transfer* on 6th September and the *Stena Freighter* replacing the *Stena Partner* in December 2010. The world had become a very different place from that when the two sets of new ships were ordered and the future would now run to a somewhat modified plan.

*The **Stena Transporter** arrives at Europort at the end of a routine crossing from Harwich. (Rob de Visser)*

*The **Stena Hollandica** (2001) pictured leaving the Hook of Holland following her jumboisation. (Rob de Visser)*

THE STENA LINE BV STORY TO DATE

Meanwhile 1st September 2010 marked 20 years of Stena Line BV on the Harwich - Hook route; years that have seen some tremendous changes. New routes have come under the control of the Hook of Holland, the futuristic HSS has been and gone, new ships have replaced old ships with a regularity that often defies belief with each arrival being both bigger and better equipped than ever before.

Yet the Harwich - Hook route still retains an affection amongst those who recall the 'old days', days of the steamers, the night boats, the boat trains, the 'Amsterdammer' and 'Windmiller' mini-trips and the mini-cruises of the 1980s. With ferry fares now cheaper, in real terms, than ever before, the old classic foot passenger is slowly returning to the route as inclusive rail and sail tickets, such as 'Dutch flyer' and 'Go London', now compete favourably with the low cost airlines.

But the bigger picture has changed and under Stena time never stands still. It remains as true today as it was in the early days – "Stena Line would not be Stena if the targets were not rather high, we have learned that the Group likes speed". Today it is freight that is by far and away the dominant consideration with the Superferries being ample proof of the way that times have changed. The additional new freight ships and replacement tonnage arriving throughout 2010 and 2011 give Stena Line BV Area North Sea a fleet of six ferries each equipped to provide a first class service.

During the last decade alone investment in Stena Line BV now totals a colossal 1.2 billion Euro and is the result of the Olsson family's earlier promise as regards new ships. That promised investment has been well and truly honoured, an achievement celebrated in June 2010 by the awarding of the CBE to Dan Sten Olsson 'in recognition of his long standing business relations with the UK'. It was presented by the Earl of Wessex in a ceremony in Stockholm on board HMS *Kent*, there for the royal wedding of the Swedish Crown Princess Victoria, a name fittingly co-incident amongst the early ships of Stena Line.

Perhaps better resourced now than ever before, Stena Line BV is indeed 'ready for the future'.

*This picture shows the **Stena Britannica** (2003) following her jumboisation on passage to the Hook of Holland from Harwich. (FotoFlite)*

CHAPTER THREE

The World's Largest Ferries

On 9th November 2006 Stena Reederi AB entered into a contract with Aker Yards ASA for two new ferries with an option for two more. Each was of a new design called 'Aker Ropax 55' whereby the 55 referred to the approximate number of 100 metre lengths of deck space given over to freight traffic, ie 5,500 metres.

To Stena Line, a Ropax 55 meant a 62,200 gross tons SuperFerry, one that could provide on-board space for around 300 lorries and 230 cars together with high quality accommodation and facilities for 1,200 passengers. The price would be 200 million Euro per ship with the contract creating a multinational link between the design teams of both Stena RoRo in Sweden and Aker Yards in Rauma, Finland. Construction would take place at Aker's two German yards in Rostock-Warnemunde and Wismar.

WORK COMMENCES

On 10th April 2008 the first of the steel plates were cut at the Warnemunde yard. The expectation at the time was that the first ship, yard number 159, would be delivered in the first quarter of 2010 and the second ship, yard number 164, would arrive around six months later.

By any method of measurement or categorisation these ships were going to be huge. At 240 metres long, 32 metres wide, a draught of 6.4 metres and a re-rated gross tonnage of 63,039 they were designed to be the world's largest combined cargo and passenger ships of their class and were thought of as being another *Stena Britannica* and *Stena Hollandica* registered in Harwich and Hook of Holland respectively.

NEW YARD OWNERS

An official ceremony to mark the laying of the first ship's keel took place at the Warnemunde yard on 22nd September 2008 when the owner of Stena AB, Dan Sten Olsson, and the Shipyard Director, Einar Brondtlund, placed the traditional lucky coin on the dock block beneath the forward section of the ship.

That same day was also a significant one for the shipyards themselves as earlier Aker Yards ASA had disposed of a controlling interest in both of them to a company called FLC West, a Russian state-controlled investment company, for the sum of 292 million Euro. The sale was completed on 29th July 2008 and on the day of this first keel-laying ceremony the two German sites were given a new name of Wadan Yards.

Over 200 guests were present as an orchestra played the national anthems of Sweden, Germany, Russia and Norway, these now being the countries variously associated with the project.

The construction of each ship was to be split between the two yards with Warnemunde responsible for the forward sections and Wismar the aft sections. The forward sections would undergo a sea tow of around 45 nautical miles to the Wismar dry dock, a huge basin 13 metres deep, 340 metres long and 67 metres wide, all housed within a covered hanger-type building hall. Here the two parts would be welded together with the wheelhouse and superstructure added later. As described by Lars Back, the shipyard Project Manager, each ship would eventually consist of around 50 giant blocks constructed on a prefabricated modular system. The 130-metre forward and bow section of yard no. 159 left Warnemunde on 25th January 2009 and two days later was floating up against the awaiting aft section in Wismar. By early March 2009 many of its building blocks were then in place, all welded together and very much looking like a ship.

*The bow section of the **Stena Hollandica** is seen here leaving the yard in Warnemunde under tow for Wismar. (Stena Line)*

*The bow section of the **Stena Hollandica** is manoeuvred into the central construction yard at Wismar prior to being joined up with the main passenger accommodation and second part of the hull. (Stena Line)*

YARD BANKRUPTCY AND DELAYS

On 5th June 2009 came a shock announcement that Wadan Yards had filed for bankruptcy amidst reports that FLC West had failed to fully invest the capital they had promised and that, according to the appointed insolvency administration company of Marc Odebrecht, they also owed various suppliers the sum of 90 million Euro.

On the following day yard no.159 was moved out of the Wismar dry dock and moored up alongside the quay pending her future outfitting and completion. At the time it was thought she was around 70% complete but the second ship, still in sections at Warnemunde, was only around 15% ready.

Summer 2009 was to see talks and negotiations aimed at rescuing the ongoing construction of the two ships. On 12th July Mandataria Finance, a Luxembourg investment company, bought out Aker's remaining interest in the yards and this was followed on 17th August by the Board of Creditors selling both yards to a Russian investor, Vitaly Yusufov, for 40.5 million Euro. The yards were once again renamed, this time to Nordic Yards.

Eventually an agreement was reached on 2nd September involving the German Government acting as 90% guarantor to a 187 million Euro Federal and private banking loan facility being granted to Nordic Yards. Initially this was dependent upon Stena taking the ships at the original contract price. However, it was later accepted that Stena would receive a reduction of 12 million Euro per ship in view of an expected three-month delay in completion with the first ship now due in either May or June 2010. It had all become 'a project too big to fail' and there was huge relief all round when production resumed on 1st October.

In the meantime the building of yard no.164 had moved on from having had her keel laid in Warnemunde on 9th July 2009 to later being readied for towing round to Wismar where she arrived on 2nd November, the day after yard no. 159 was moved out of the building hall.

POOR MARKET AND FINANCES

The financial difficulties endured by the shipyards were part of a global economic crisis which escalated in 2008, the effects of which had not been seen for many a decade. The UK was to endure a pronounced recession longer than most other countries with the result that freight to and from the Continent became severely depressed. On the Harwich-Hook route the number of freight units carried in 2008 was 160,000 and by 2009 it had fallen to just 138,000. As a consequence it was decided that there would be a change to the sequence of ship deployment.

At the time there was no demand for the largest freight capacity to be on the evening crossings from the Hook, as was the case at the time of the order in December 2006, but there was an increasing demand for a larger passenger capacity on evening crossings from Harwich. Thus it was decided to re-designate yard no.159 to become the new *Stena Hollandica* and yard no 164 would instead become the next *Stena Britannica*.

As regards freight, the situation was suggesting to Pim de Lange a need to reduce capacity throughout the industry in general and/or to rationalise if the ro-ro sector was to again become overall a healthy and profitable one. However, he argued that larger ships could be operationally more efficient. This point was reiterated by Bo Severed, CEO at Stena RoRo, who said that these new ships were not only the right ships to invest in but North Sea routes were also the right routes in which to invest.

To help ease the financial strain on Stena Line BV, Stena AB agreed to waive their charter fees for a year and temporarily reduce the capital cost of the ships. This was in recognition of the delays into service and an ongoing recessionary situation that made little immediate business sense in introducing such huge new ferries to a weak market. Based on the maximum design loading of around 300 freight units per crossing, carryings in early 2010 were running at only a third of the route's projected capacity as traffic continued to show little cause for optimism. Once again, as Pim de Lange said at the time, it was a case of 'we can count ourselves lucky in the fact that we are part of a strong group with a dedicated owner'.

FINISHING TOUCHES

During the first week of February 2010, after three months outside, the now future *Stena Hollandica* was brought back inside the Wismar covered dry dock and placed alongside *Stena Britannica* still under construction. Both ships were then resting on blocks with their hulls just 60 cm apart! Conditions were much more amenable inside the hall as the outside temperature was regularly between -5⁰C and -8⁰C and this certainly made the job of painting the ship a little easier. At times up to 300 workers were employed solely in painting the freight decks.

On 21st March the *Stena Hollandica* re-emerged from the building hall though as yet with no name on her hull. By 25th March she was proudly displaying a freshly painted name as she was presented to a group of around 30 press and media representatives. Then at 16.30 the following day she left Wismar for her first sea trials. These were technical

trials in order to test and fine-tune the main engines and associated machinery as well as trial run the cabin accommodation. She sailed around the area between Rugen and Bornholm before arriving back at Wismar in the evening of 28th March.

A month later came her official trials when on 21st April she left for three days of intensive ship handling and manoeuvring along with a full range of navigation, fire and on-board safety tests. Some 300 dock and company employees were on board throughout, all helping to further test the impressive galley facilities. On 25th April she had a day of inclining tests inside the building hall. This meant moving the *Stena Britannica* to lay up outside, very much looking in need of the five months of work still to be done on her.

FLAG DAYS

Having been built and delivered to Stena RoRo under the Swedish flag, the *Stena Hollandica* was handed over in Wismar to her new operators, Stena Line BV, on 7th May 2010. She was accordingly re-flagged to the Dutch flag under the command of Captain Laas van der Zee before leaving Wismar at 16.00 on 10th May for her delivery voyage to the Hook. She sailed there via Harwich where she passed the outward bound *Stena Partner* and *Stena Britannica* close by Felixstowe before undergoing berthing trials between 09.30 and 11.45 on 12th May. She later left to arrive at the Hook at 22.00 the same day and was then laid up at the Damen Yard in Rotterdam for final fitting out, storing and crew familiarisation.

The 'old' *Stena Hollandica* made her final voyage from Harwich on the night of 15th May. After arriving at the

An impressive view of the **Stena Hollandica** *completely scaffolded in the latter part of her construction. (Stena Line)*

*The **Stena Hollandica** being towed out of the covered construction yard during June 2009. (Stena Line)*

Hook the next morning she then left directly for the Remontowa yard in Poland. The 'new' *Stena Hollandica* had earlier that morning left the Damen yard, sailed out to sea and was heading back in towards her berth at the Hook resulting in the only occasion the two ships met as they passed by each other inside the New Waterway. The maiden voyage of the new ship was to Harwich on the scheduled 14.30 sailing that same day. The 'old' *Stena Hollandica* arrived in Gdansk in the early morning of 19th May to undergo a major refit.

The official naming day of the *Stena Hollandica* took place at the Hook on 8th June 2010 in the presence of HRH Prinses Margriet of Holland and around 400 guests.

STENA BRITANNICA PROGRESS

The construction, trials and testing arrangements of the *Stena Britannica* followed a similar pattern to that of her sister ship and she was eventually handed over to Stena RoRo on 28th September 2010. The following day she was transferred to Stena Line BV and changed to the British flag. She then sailed from Wismar on 2nd October to arrive at a wet and dismal Harwich for berthing trials on the morning of 4th October. In doing so she passed by the *Stena Carrier*, recently introduced to the Harwich - Rotterdam route, and then her former namesake, (earlier renamed simply as *Britannica* on 21st September) a little upstream from Landguard Point just as the *Stena Hollandica* had done in May. She was at Harwich between 09.30 and 13.30 after which she left for the Hook and was then laid up in Rotterdam for her own sequence of storing and familiarisation.

Her first commercial sailing was from the Hook of Holland on the 22.00 overnight crossing on 9th October 2010. The *Britannica* made her last crossing on the route, day boat ex Harwich, also on the 9th thereafter leaving the Hook on the morning of the 10th for Poland and her own refit.

The official naming ceremony of the 'new' *Stena Britannica* took place at Harwich on 19th October by the wife of Mr Philip Hammond, the UK Secretary of State for Transport. For the benefit of invited guests there was an afternoon lunch cruise of around two hours between 14.00 and 16.00 following which she then made a very late departure from Harwich at around 17.00 to the Hook with the intention of a quick trip and a quick turn round in order to pick up her normal schedule the next day.

TERMINAL BERTHS

Neither Harwich nor the Hook had previously possessed any double-deck loading berths and thus there was now a need to provide them.

Early in 2008 the Swedish firm TTS Port Equipment AB, part of TTS Marine ASA of Bergen, Norway was chosen by Stena Line BV to provide a suitable capability at the Hook. The contract price was 4 million Euro. In order to minimise any service disruption it was decided to utilise and convert the existing lower deck linkspan with much of the work being carried out at night.

The old twin support and overhead gantry berth had used motor-driven counterweights and a wire system for raising and lowering the ramp. This was replaced with two open frame towers equipped with hydraulic cylinders. A manual operation mode enables staff to set the level of the lower deck linkspan according to the ship's draft and water level. Once the linkspan is locked into place, an automatic system then monitors and follows any tidal variations and ship movements.

A new upper deck linkspan and ramp uses the existing lower ramp structure as a supporting base and is designed to align with the centre line of the new ships. A vehicular access ramp runs up from quay level on the seaward side of the lower deck and onto the adjustable upper ramp which is raised using the hydraulic cylinders built inside the two new towers. A total of 1,150 tonnes of old structure, counterweights, motors and lifting gear were removed with only 500 tonnes of new equipment being needed in its place. The new span, which was made in China, arrived in September 2009 and after the preparatory work had been completed it was lifted into place in October.

At Harwich, TTS were also awarded a linkspan contract to be carried out throughout early 2010. This was agreed on 16th December 2009 and worth NOK38 million though here a wholly different type of structure, again made in China, was required from that at the Hook.

A new 120-metre long upper deck ramp and linkspan, elevated by means of hydraulic cylinders built into and dropping down from within an arched tubular support structure, was placed above the existing no.2 Berth. This arch was lifted into position in late March 2010 by a floating crane and spans the roadway below. It rests on new dolphin supports that are completely separate from the existing pontoon that continues to provide access to the lower deck, the seaward end of which was modified slightly to improve berthing access. The approach road to the upper deck runs off the old access apron to the adjacent former HSS berth.

At each port the upper deck linkspan rests upon the ship with normal operations seeing both vessels berth stern in at the Hook and bow in at Harwich.

FREIGHT DECKS

The total length of lane metreage is arranged throughout a sequence of four odd numbered decks.

The lowest deck, Lower cargo Deck 1, is really Deck 2 or the Tank Top Deck and has 445 metres of space. Above this is a main Deck 3 with 1,695 metres, an upper main Deck 5 with 1,740 metres and a second upper deck or top Deck 7 of 1,620 metres. The free height, or clearance height, on all these decks is set at 4.8 metres though the aft end of Deck 7 is open deck.

The ships have full drive through to shore capability at both ends utilising, for the first time on the route, double-deck loading berths with twin ramps. The main Deck 3 is accessed via a 21 x 7 metre internally stowed bow ramp and a stern ramp measuring 16 x 17 metres. Both have a clearance height of 5 metres. The second entrance / exit is via the upper main Deck 5 where at the forward end a shore-based ramp rests on the upper bow section. Here a 7 metre wide roadway leads out from a hinged doorway in the forward superstructure, across the deck and through a 5 metre high aperture, created when a 'visor' section of the upper bow is raised, and then onto a matching width shore ramp. Access at the stern similarly connects with another shore-based resting ramp, this one being much wider at around 17 metres.

Cargo Deck 1 is five lanes wide whilst the greater parts of the other three cargo decks are nine lanes wide, five on the starboard side and four on the port side of a partitioning support casing. These reduce by one lane width in areas restricted by either the lifeboats on both sides of Deck 7 or, on the other decks, by the exhaust housing which is located one lane to the port-side of centre. The freight lanes are set at 3.1 metres wide though several of the very innermost and outermost lanes narrow to 2.9 metres wide.

On the port side of Deck 3 is a hoistable mezzanine Car Deck 4. Here there are five car lanes, each 2.4 metres wide, that fit in above the space of four lorry lanes on Deck 3 below. In total there are 729 car lane metres, sufficient for 146 cars, with four lanes running the entire deck length with a smaller recess lane nearest the centre line.

Internal ramps, both fixed and tilting, connect the various decks. Deck 1 has fixed single lane centre ramps forward and aft to Deck 3 measuring 40 by 3.5 metres whilst on the starboard side of Deck 3 is a single lane tiltable ramp, ie two way, to and from Deck 5 that measures 50 by 3.2 metres. On the port side a double lane tiltable ramp, 51 x 6 metres, links Decks 5 and 7. All ramps have a height clearance of 4.8 metres. On-board turning circles on the main freight decks vary between 13 metres and 14.9 metres radius. In the case of a linkspan failure at either level it remains possible to fully load and unload the ships using a combination of their internal ramps to bring cargo to the relevant shore ramp.

Certain freight lanes are as long as the overall length of either the *Stena Trader* or *Stena Traveller* whilst one main freight deck on its own can carry well in excess of an entire passenger ferry of just a few years ago. In total, including the car deck, each ship might carry around 25 times its own length in freight and cars. Total deadweight is 11,600 tonnes. Temperature-controlled cargo is catered for by the provision of 185 refrigerated sockets.

ENGINES

In April 2007 the MAN Diesel Group of Augsburg Germany became the suppliers of the ships' main on-board power plant and equipment. Each have four main engines of the MAN 48/60CR medium speed common rail fuel injection type which provide 1200 kW per cylinder at 500rpm. There are two 8-cylinder 8L engines each rated at 9600 kW output, plus two 6 cylinder 6L engines, each rated at 7200 kW. These are assembled as two sets, using one of each engine, in a 'father and son' arrangement connected by a twin input shaft single output shaft double reduction Renk gearbox. Total propulsive power is 33,600kW or 46,000hp.

The engines offer improved combustion and reduced fuel usage, examples being that on day sailings to Harwich all four main engines are in use at 85% capacity using up to 7,000 litres of heavy fuel oil per hour to provide speeds of up to 25 knots whilst on the overnight service to Hook only the two smaller main engines are needed for a more leisurely crossing of 19 knots. Although consumption varies upon the time of crossing and the time difference between each country, overall each ship consumes an average of 65 tonnes per 24 hours.

The auxiliary engines are MAN Diesel GenSets consisting of 1 7L21/31 of 1540 kW output plus 3 6L21/31's providing 1,320 kW each. All main and auxiliary engines are resiliently mounted. Additional equipment includes 2 x 3,100 kW MAN shaft generators, 2 x 5.2 metre MAN Alphatronic controllable pitch propellers driven off 41 metre shaft lines, 2 Wartsila bow thrusters each rated at 3,100 kW, 2 flap-type Becker rudders plus fin stabilisers provided by Mitsubishi.

The engine control room is situated port side on Deck 2, slightly above the level of the lowest freight deck, and somewhat unusually is provided with its own porthole!

Top: *A view of the completed* **Stena Hollandica** *en-route to Holland. (Stena Line)*

Above: *All the public areas are found throughout the whole of Deck 9. Pictured here is the Magazine Lounge, located at the aft end. (Stena Line)*

Right: *At the forward end of Deck 9 is the 'Commercial Zone' where the main dining areas are located. This picture features the self service counters of the 'Taste Restaurant' which offer a wide range of meal options. (Stena Line)*

With consideration for the environment, the engines are capable of making invisible smoke and are linked to catalysts that further reduce any emissions. Additional features include the ships being provided with shore-based power connections, via a new installation at the Hook of Holland, so as to reduce the use of engines when alongside whilst at sea the exhaust gases are directed through a heat exchanger in order to heat the interior spaces. A further opportunity to save on engine use comes from having many of the outside windows treated with a heat-reflecting film which reduces the need for air conditioning on hot days. All such features are in line with Blue Wave environmental initiatives which even extend to being able to recycle cardboard, glass and food waste.

Located on both sides of Deck 7 are two lifeboats and a fast rescue craft while a Marine Evacuation System of escape chutes and inflatable rafts is also fitted.

PUBLIC SPACES

Since the ending of the HSS service, the route's overall character has changed back towards the cruise ferry days of the 1980s. Gunnar Blomdahl, CEO of Stena Line, thought that having made the right strategic decision to take the HSS *Stena Discovery* out of service in 2007 there was a need to adapt and cater for a new 'type' of passenger, one who was spending more time on board the lengthened and renovated *Stena Britannica* and *Stena Hollandica* than they did on the HSS. 'We have to offer these new customers excellent service. They should be able to have a great time. I don't mean we should be providing entertainment, but we should offer our guests the same facilities as a first class hotel, an excellent restaurant, unexpected service with a smile, no pains should be spared for our customers'.

To achieve those goals Stena again turned to the Swedish architectural firm of Figura whose architect, Richard Nilsson, had been involved with the interior re-design of the route's existing stretched ferries. He explained that the overall aim was to create a light and modern feel based upon a contemporary Scandinavian design. Materials and fittings were all to be light and polished with the furniture using light woods with vibrant colours throughout. Stena palette reds and blues were to be the dominant fabric colours with the new ships incorporating design ambitions that would both enhance the image of the route as well as retaining an overall Swedish feel.

However, one aspect of Stena Line BV having introduced so many new, modified or updated ships in so relatively short a space of time is in showing passengers any step-change improvements to the furnishings and fittings. The answer was to give these ships a 'concept makeover' and thus in conjunction with Stena in both Gothenburg and the Hook, Figura split the ship into zones along their length and produced a linear concept with three distinct areas of roughly equal size based upon 'Commercial', 'Retail' and 'Recreational' considerations.

All the public areas are located throughout the whole of Deck 9. This deck and those above are 'only' 30 metres wide as Deck 7 tapers slightly by about a metre either side.

At the forward end is the 'Commercial' zone of the concept and here is found the main wining and dining area dominated by the 238-seater centrally located 'Taste Restaurant'. This self-service buffet provides full breakfast, lunch and dinner facilities and is flanked by various other smaller outlets. In the forward port corner is a 28-seat speciality 'Wine Bar' serving quality wines and champagnes behind which in the very far corner is a small 'Casino' area. Slightly aft of the 'Wine Bar' is the 'Metropolitan a la carte Restaurant', a sectioned off area that offers a more relaxed and upmarket style of dining for up to 118 customers.

On the starboard side is the 'Riva Bar', comprising of a Stena in-house designed bar counter that resembles an old Riva style speedboat from the 1950s. Here there are 52 seats alongside of which, in the forward starboard corner, is the oddly-sited 39 seat 'Riva Lounge', the only area set aside for smoking on board other than on the outside decks. Next to the bar is the 'Gorgeous George' Kidszone play area.

The midships section of Deck 9 contains the 'Retail' zone. This houses the Reception Desk, restyled as the 'Guest Service Desk', a 'Bureau de Change', the 'Stena Shopping' centre, a 182 seat 'C-View Lounge' plus space for a 'Teen Town' and 'Gaming Machine Area'. All are located on the starboard side of centre with the 'C-View Lounge' having access to a coffee and light snacks facility at the Guest Services Desk.

Most of this remaining midships section is occupied on the port side by a 300 square metre galley which connects at its forward end with the a la carte restaurant and at its aft end with a 307 seat 'Truckers Restaurant, Bar and Lounge'. The spaciousness of this area devoted to lorry drivers reflects the fact that the Harwich-Hook route is unique amongst long haul ferry routes in that it has a much higher ratio of freight accompanied by a driver. Something in the region of 75-80% of traffic is driven as compared to 35% on Stena Line BV's two freight routes and often less than this within the industry in general.

This 'Truckers Section' takes up the whole of the port side area given over to the 'Recreational' zone. Here Figura have worked around what they term the 'Living Room' concept, the idea being that anyone can sit and relax, look out of the window, read from a selection of free magazines, watch television or surf the internet just like being in a living room at home. Accordingly the starboard side is split by a central aisle which has on its inside a 50 seat 'Cinema', a television 'Newsroom', a 'Meeting Room' for business meetings and an 'Internet Room'. Free wi-fi is available throughout the ship. On the outer side is a 48 seat 'Stena Plus Lounge' where for an additional charge one can relax in comfort and enjoy a range of complimentary drinks and magazines provided by the adjacent 'Barista Bar'. This outlet, named after Stena Line's own coffee brand, also serves drinks and light snacks to the nearby 60 seat 'Magazine Lounge'.

Furthest most aft is access to the limited area of outside deck and the 'Sundeck Bar', a feature new to the route that is open when fine weather permits.

Passengers are free to sit anywhere in all areas throughout the ship, except the a la carte section, without any compulsion to purchase food or drinks if they choose not to.

A separate kennel room is provided, off the port side stairwell on Deck 8, for those wishing to make use of the Pets Passport scheme for dogs, cats or ferrets!

Top left: *A wide range of quality cabins are available. Shown here is an outside 2 berth Comfort Class cabin. Note the complimentary mini-bar. (Stena Line)*

Top right: *A notably impressive feature of the Superferries are their 'Truckers Restaurant, Bar and Lounges' which are for the exclusive use of freight drivers only. (Stena Line)*

Above: *The Stena Plus Lounge where passengers can relax whilst enjoying a higher standard of comfort and service. (Stena Line)*

Right: *Shown here is the 'Metropolitan a la carte Restaurant' offering a more upmarket dining experience. (Stena Line)*

CABINS

A further concept change was to abolish the idea of cabins and to reclassify such accommodation as rooms, all equipped with satellite television! This combines Stena's first class hotel idea with a more cruise-like travel experience.

A total of 538 rooms are situated throughout Decks 10 and 11 with 276 being on Deck 10 and 262 on Deck 11. They are all en-suite and variously range from quality standard class to high-class luxury level suites. A total of 237 rooms are set aside for the exclusive use of drivers whilst the others consist of 166 standard inside twin, 2 disabled inside, 33 standard outside twin, 59 standard outside 5 berth, 30 Comfort Class, 9 Captains Class and 2 top of the range Captains Suites. Inside rooms have a floor space of 8.5 square metres, outside rooms have 9.5 square metres, outside 5 berth, Comfort and Captain's Class have 11.5 square metres whilst the Suites are a very spacious 27.5 square metres. All rooms have beds from the luxury Swedish design of DUX whilst many of the outside rooms are improved by the provision of a 1200 mm wide lower berth with nothing narrower than 900 mm in all the others, including the newly described Pullman berths, formerly known as either the upper or drop down bunks. The wider 1200 mm berths have enough space for two small children and provide the extra berth in 5 berth rooms highly suited for families.

All outside rooms are fitted with larger windows than usual with many having an impressive 1-metre diameter porthole whilst the wardrobes have been trimmed back in size to further enhance a sense of spaciousness. The room door key-cards are used for switching the electricity on or off inside the cabins via a specially designed key holder labelled 'Hotel Card'. The higher grades of accommodation, Comfort and Captain Class, are provided with mini-bars

*The **Stena Britannica** was named by Mrs Susan Hammond (right) wife of the UK's Secretary of State for Transport, Philip Hammond (left) at a ceremony at Harwich on 19th October 2010. (John Hendy)*

whilst the two Suites, located on both forward wings of Deck 10, are extremely well equipped with separated bedroom and lounge areas, large flat screen television and full mini-bar with complimentary bottles of champagne.

Quality fittings are evident throughout the ships and the

*This view of Deck 3 looking aft illustrates one of three such decks in the **Stena Britannica**. (John Hendy)*

The **Stena Hollandica** makes an impressive view as she rounds Landguard Point before entering Harwich Haven from the Hook of Holland. *(Ian Boyle)*

*This interesting view shows the **Stena Britannica** (2003) and **Stena Hollandica** passing each other in the Stour on the 'Hollandica's' first visit to Harwich. (Ian Boyle)*

sense of on-board space is quite noticeable. The stairway landings are decorated with coloured montages of selected tourist sites and iconic figures whilst the cabin corridors feature black and white photographs depicting a travel and leisure activities theme.

All the crew accommodation is located on Bridge Deck 12. Here there are 85 outside cabins together with an officer and crew mess room, separate crew and officer dayrooms, a staff conference room and mini gymnasium. Five Captain Class cabins provide 1 for the Master and 4 for the Senior Officers whilst 11 Officer Class cabins are for Junior Officers. A further 69 cabins for the rest of the crew are all single occupancy.

The topmost deck, Deck 13, is the helicopter deck at a height of 38.4 metres above BL or 32 metres above the waterline.

HOOKING HARWICH UP WITH HOLLAND

The *Stena Hollandica* and *Stena Britannica* were ordered at a time when demand on certain days of the week would often overwhelm the capacity of the route. However, the years of plenty that led up to 2008 were followed by a significant downturn in 2009 and on into 2010 which made the ships appear somewhat out of place when first introduced into service. Their main customers are increasingly the major UK supermarkets though as the economy improves so the capacity will be there to attract a more diverse range of cargo. However, in line with the industry in general, it is not expected that the traffic levels of 2008 will return much before 2012 no doubt aided by the attraction and demands of the London Olympics. It is fair to say that these ships would not have been built had it been known just how badly those global economic woes would develop but they were 'Designed for the future, for the passengers of today'. As such they are excellent ships for 'Hooking Harwich up with Holland' and in time will no doubt prove to have been a most opportune investment.

*The **Stena Britannica** was delivered to Stena Line in October 2010. She is seen here outward bound to the Hook of Holland on her morning service from the UK. (Ian Boyle)*

Stena Hollandica (Miles Cowsill)

CHAPTER FOUR

Building on the Success of the New Ships

HARWICH - HOOK

Since 2010, following the introduction of the *Stena Hollandica* and *Stena Britannica*, the Harwich to Hook of Holland route was to enjoy a decade of stability and sustained reliability. These two Superferries (63039gt., 240m), continued the traditional day-boat night-boat service except for times when one or the other went away for their periodic dry-docking. During such times the route would drop down to a one ship service and any excess vehicle and trailer traffic diverted onto freight only sailings operating via Rotterdam (Europoort). Only rarely was a relief ship has been brought in.

In October 2012 the *Stena Britannica* underwent an extended period in dry-dock with her sailings then covered by the *Stena Hollandica*. Those of the *Stena Hollandica* were in turn covered by the *Stena Hibernia* (13,017gt., 142.50m.) between 29th September and 10th October. This ship, with a capacity for 110 trailers, had been brought out of lay-up in Belfast to run freight only sailings to the Hook. Several years later, in January 2020, when both Superferries were in turn receiving consecutive refits, their respective sailings were covered by the 158 trailer freight ship *Misida* (15586gt., 165.75m.), this ship having been moved off Stena Line's Rotterdam to Killingholme route.

Both Superferries retain the title of being the world's largest ro-ro ferries and although still thoroughly modern in design they have, like many others, been faced with ever more stringent environmental and green power demands with various initiatives having been imposed aimed at reducing pollution levels. A shore-power facility, designed to cut down on running ships engines when alongside, was installed at the

Hook of Holland in conjunction with contractor ABB and officially opened on 13th June 2012. (In March 2015, the former *Stena Hollandica*, now the *Stena Germanica*, became the world's first commercial marine vessel to run trialling methanol as a primary fuel.)

One major demand was that ships either use more expensive low sulphur fuels or fit cleaner exhaust gas technologies. Here Stena Line chose to fit a pioneering in-line closed-loop system designed by Wartsila, a system generally referred to as scrubbers. These fit around the funnel and clean up the exhaust gases by using wash water to remove the sulphurous emissions. The very first to have this system fitted was the *Stena Transit* in October 2015. The *Stena Britannica* had hers fitted whilst dry docking at Damen Shipyard Rotterdam between 31st October and 12th November 2016 and the *Stena Hollandica* likewise when in dry dock between 21st February and 10th March 2017.

A major change at Hook of Holland came with the retirement of Pim de Lange as Stena Line B.V.'s Managing Director on 1st January 2014. After almost 18 years in charge he commented that more had happened in that time than in the previous hundred years. Stena Line had moved from being just one of the players to a major player on the North Sea as he admitted having 'approached my work with a great drive and passion, as if it was my own company. For me, it was a sort of life's work with a strong desire to turn it into a strong and healthy company. And that required a great number of sacrifices. But it was ultimately all worthwhile, because together we succeeded'. His successor was Annika Hult, formerly the M.D. of Stena International in Luxembourg. Sadly, Pim de Lange passed away on 14th March 2016.

*The **Stena Scandinavica** (ex **Stena Britannica**) arrives at Gothenburg on her overnight sailing from Germany in September 2019. (Miles Cowsill)*

*The **Stena Germanica** (ex **Stena Hollandica**) swings off the berth at Gothenburg on her 14 hour sailing to Keil. (Miles Cowsill)*

HOOK - KILLINGHOLME

Stena Line's major presence on the North Sea consists not only Harwich - Hook but a number of other services as well, primarily for freight. Since opening on 9th October 2000 the Hook - Killingholme route has been hugely successful and in similar fashion to Harwich - Hook it has also enjoyed the benefit and reliability of two large and brand new sister ships.

The *Stena Transporter*, (34,700gt., 212m), first entered service on 1st March 2011, displacing the chartered *Finnarrow*, (25996gt., 168m), whilst the *Stena Transit* entered service on 7th November 2011, displacing the chartered *Coraggio*, (24,950gt., 199.14m). Sailings then regularly departed the Hook at 21.00 (20.30 Saturday/Sunday) to arrive at Killingholme at 06.45 with return sailings departing at 20.30, arriving back at the Hook at 09.00.

These twin Samsung built vessels each cost Euro 110m. and have a capacity for 260 freight units and up to 300 passengers, ie lorry drivers. They were each celebrated at the Hook of Holland by way of Naming Days - the *Stena Transporter* on 19th April 2011 by Dutch Minister Melanie Schultz van Haegen and the *Stena Transit* by Jeannette Baljeu, Deputy Mayor of Rotterdam, on 15th November.

The *Stena Transit* went on to become the world's first recipient of the innovative Wartsila scrubber system when dry-docked at Damen Shiprepair Amsterdam between 2nd and 12th October 2015 with the Stena Transporter being similarly fitted out between 4th and 14th March 2016. The *Stena Transit* was the last piece of a ship jigsaw which, during the previous 5 years, had seen Stena Line invest well over 1 Billion Euros in their North Sea services.

ROTTERDAM - HARWICH

Whilst the pieces fell easily into place on the two principal routes at the Hook of Holland, others were having great difficulty being fitted in at Rotterdam Europoort. In late 2010 the Rotterdam to Harwich route was due to see the *Stena Transfer* and *Stena Partner* (each 21,162gt., 184.61m., 180 trailers), replaced by two larger capacity freight ships, the *Stena Carrier* and *Stena Freighter*, (each 21,104gt., 183m., 225 trailers).

Both the 'Carrier' and 'Freighter' had been made redundant at the end of August following Stena Line's closure of their Gothenburg to Travemunde freight service, this being the result of Stena having decided to concentrate traffic on their Gothenburg to Kiel service via a doubling of its route capacity. This was to be achieved by the introduction of the former Harwich vessels, *Stena Hollandica* and *Stena Britannica*, respectively re-named the *Stena Germanica* and *Stena Scandinavica*.

On 6th September 2010 the *Stena Transfer* was replaced by the *Stena Carrier* whilst the *Stena Partner* was scheduled to remain at Harwich a little longer until the *Stena Freighter* replaced her in December. Unfortunately, on 9th November, a fire broke out onboard the *Stena Scandinavica* during her refit in Gdansk. This greatly delayed her return to service and also the release of the *Stena Freighter* which had since been deployed between Gothenburg and Kiel. As a result the *Stena Partner* was instead replaced, on 20th December 2010, by the *Ark Forwarder*, sister ship to both the *Stena Carrier* and *Stena Freighter*. She remained on the route for four months until the Stena Freighter finally arrived on 26th April 2011.

However these twin replacement vessels proved too big, and too expensive to run, during a period of general over capacity amongst several competing North Sea routes. Locally Harwich had competition in the form of a Rotterdam to Ipswich service operated by CLdN/Cobelfret. This company was running two newly built freight ships, the *Capucine* and *Severine*, (16,342gt., 152m), each with a capacity for 140 trailers. However, on 3rd August 2012 Cobelfret announced that due to a poor financial situation they would be closing this route on 17th August. Very quickly, on 6th August, Stena Line made an approach as regards taking the ships over and this resulted in Cobelfret agreeing to a five year bareboat charter.

*The **Stena Forerunner** pictured leaving the Hook of Holland in 2019. (Rob de Visser)*

The **Stena Britannica** pictured following the insulation of her scrubber units in 2016. (Rob de Visser)

The two ships were better suited to Stena Line's current operations and the prevailing market conditions. They were much cheaper to run and so, on 3rd September 2012, the single engined *Capucine* and *Severine* replaced the four-engined *Stena Carrier* and *Stena Freighter*.

Soon afterwards this once loss making route became more stable and financially secure and this led to a period of investment in Europoort's ageing facilities. A contract was signed on 18th July 2013 between Stena Line and the Port of Rotterdam in order to renew the quay wall and replace the linkspan. However, when part way through the works, it was decided to expand the redevelopment still further and thus when finished the quay was now 212 metres long with not one but two linkspan berths, one of which was slightly angled into the quay wall. The total cost was Euro 24m. and officially opened in February 2018.

In July 2017 it was announced that the Rotterdam to Harwich route would receive a pair of replacement vessels in January 2018, rumoured to be the *Misana* and *Misidi*. However as part of an overall plan to better provision the company's North Sea routes these ships were instead put onto the Rotterdam to Killingholme service. This meant that when the *Capucine* and *Severine* both went off charter in late December 2017 the Harwich route would lose the benefit of a sister ship operation. A twice a day service was still required but since January 2018 various ships appeared in all shapes and sizes.

The first replacement to arrive was the *Stena Scotia* (13,017gt., 142.5m.) as from 4th January and she was then partnered by the *Stena Forerunner* (24688gt., 195.3m), which arrived on 12th January. In June 2018 the *Stena Forerunner* left and was replaced by the *Mistral* (10,471gt., 153.45m) between 2nd June and 21st August following which the *Mistral* was in turn replaced by the *Bore Bay* (10,572gt., 138.5m), which took up sailings on 19th August.

Around this time the *Stena Scotia* then left and her replacement was the *Misana*, off the Killingholme route, from mid August until mid September. The *Misana* then partnered the *Bore Bay* until the final arrival that year of the *Somerset*, (21,005gt., 183.4m), on charter from Cobelfret. This vessel arrived on 19th September and the *Misana* was then released back to Killingholme.

The *Somerset* and *Bore Bay* partnership lasted until 26th February 2019 when the *Bore Bay* was replaced by the *Misana* making a second appearance at Harwich. In late February 2020, following the end of her charter, the *Misana* then left Harwich and was replaced by a reappearance of the Stena Forerunner.

ROTTERDAM - KILLINGHOLME

The above mentioned route between Rotterdam Europoort and Killingholme became a fourth route to be operated by Stena Line B.V. and was opened on 2nd September 2014. This was as a result of the ongoing success of the route between the Hook of Holland and Killingholme. Demand was such that both the *Stena Transporter* and *Stena Transit* were often fully booked and thus an 'overflow' route was required. It was to be freight only, offering additional capacity for unaccompanied trailers, and was inaugurated by the *Stena Scotia* (13,017gt., 142.5m) which was on charter from Stena Ro-Ro. Able to carry 110 x 12m trailers she made three round trips per week departing Rotterdam each Tuesday, Thursday and Sunday at 17.00 and from Killingholme each Monday, Wednesday and Saturday at 22.00.

As demand gradually increased a second ship, the *Caroline Russ* (10,488gt., 153.45m), was added on 31st October 2016. Sailings were then doubled to six per week with the *Caroline Russ* (sister ship to the *Mistral*) handling up to 102 x 12m trailers.

The change of plan to the July 2017 announcement that new ships would be going to Killingholme instead of Harwich caused the *Stena Scotia* and *Caroline Russ* to replaced, on 4th January 2018, by the 158 trailer capacity sister ships, *Misana* and *Misida* (15,586gt., 165.75m.), then on charter to Stena Ro-Ro. Their arrival coincided with the new berth and terminal facilities being opened at Europoort.

The *Stena Scotia* was moved onto the Harwich service and whilst the new ships were not intended to be at Harwich they did, at one time or other, see service there. In March 2019 the *Misana* was moved to spend what became the next 12 months on the Rotterdam to Harwich route when she replaced the *Bore Bay*. At Killingholme her sailings were taken over by the *Stena Forerunner*. As mentioned earlier, the *Misida* was at Harwich in January 2020 acting as cover for when the two Superferries were away on refits. A short term replacement for the *Misida* was the *Stena Nordica* from 13th to 22nd January.

*A powerful view of the **Stena Hollandica** in dry-dock at Damen Schiedam, Rotterdam. (Rob de Visser)*

*The **Stena Hollandica** arrives at the Hook of Holland in February 2020. (Rob de Visser)*

When their respective charters ended the *Misana* and *Misida* were replaced by another pair of freight ships, the much larger *Hatche* and *Qezban* (29,004gt., 193m). These 240 trailer capacity vessels were again on charter, from Alternative Transport of Istanbul, and both were placed on the Rotterdam to Killingholme route. The *Hatche* entered service on 28th January 2020 and the *Qezban* on 8th March. The arrival of the *Qezban* then saw the *Stena Forerunner* moved back to the Harwich route, replacing the *Misana*, sailing opposite the *Somerset*. Overall these new ships and route changes gave the services out of Rotterdam Europoort a 25% increase in capacity.

COVID-19 AND BEYOND

In early 2020 the shipping industry, and the world in general, was hit by a devastating virus - Covid-19. Almost immediately the industry went into recession with each company making their own arrangements that either saw ships laid up and/or staff laid off, sometimes permanently. By the end of April 2020 the *Stena Forerunner* and *Hatche* were laid up as the Rotterdam services were reduced to just the one ship sailing alternate days. Routes from the Hook of Holland were maintained for as long as was feasible for freight and for essential travel only.

Just as the world had become a very different place from when the two sets of new ships were ordered over a decade ago, so too, at the start of the 2020's, did the world become a wholly different place yet again. However, Stena Line have always had an eye on the future, though never envisaging the disaster through which that future now lay. At the opening of the Hook's shore power installation back in June 2012, Minister Melanie Schultz van Haegen said 'To me, Stena Line is a company that radiates daring and dynamism. A company that retains loyal customers and achieves positive results, even in less prosperous times'.

When 'normal' returns, Stena Line North Sea will no doubt maintain the ships it needs to play its part in 'Connecting Europe, for a sustainable future' and with Harwich - Hook still at the forefront of North Sea travel.

*The winter sun catches the **Stena Britannica** as she arrives at the Hook of Holland in January 2020. This view shows the re-design of her funnel markings, which improved the apperance of both sisters. (Rob de Visser)*

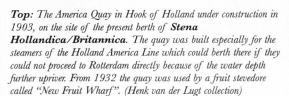

Top: The America Quay in Hook of Holland under construction in 1903, on the site of the present berth of **Stena Hollandica/Britannica**. The quay was built especially for the steamers of the Holland America Line which could berth there if they could not proceed to Rotterdam directly because of the water depth further upriver. From 1932 the quay was used by a fruit stevedore called "New Fruit Wharf". (Henk van der Lugt collection)

Above left: The Hook van Holland Railway Station and Harwich Quay seen from the lighthouse around 1900. There is no ship alongside as until 1904 the ships only berthed shortly at Hook of Holland allowing the passengers to transfer to the international trains. (Henk van der Lugt collection)

Above right: The Hook of Holland Railway Station and Harwich Quay around 1910. Clearly visible is the short distance from the platform to the ship. However, until 1986, passengers transferring from the trains to the ships or vice versa were given no protection from the elements. (Henk van der Lugt collection)

Right: An electric train about to depart from the Hook of Holland Railway Station in the 1950s. Looking at the man in uniform on the platform it is probably a military train connecting with the troopships which operated between Harwich and Hook of Holland between 1945 and 1961. (Henk van der Lugt collection)

Top Left: *During the first World War the service between Hook of Holland and Harwich came to a standstill although an irregular service between Tilbury and Rotterdam (via Hook of Holland) was maintained. The photo shows the* **Brussels** *alongside at the Hook of Holland during the First World War, but also gives an idea of the scale of operations in these days. (Henk van der Lugt collection)*

Top right: *The* **Prague** *alongside at the Hook of Holland in the early 1930s. The crane in the foreground is one of the original steam cranes. The limited outreach of these cranes caused problems with the cargo handling on the ships of the 'Vienna' class which were larger than their predecessors. Hence new electric cranes were put on the quay in the 1930's and one of these can be seen to the left. (Henk van der Lugt collection)*

Above: *Specially for the introduction of the* **Koningin Beatrix** *a new berth was constructed in Hook of Holland on the site of the former Fruitwharf. On this view of 22nd July 1989 the covered walkway for footpassengers is clearly visible. The international train in the foreground is one of the last remains of an era during which several places in Europe and even Moscow could be reached from Hook of Holland by train. (Henk van der Lugt collection)*

Right: *A view from the stern of* **Koningin Beatrix** *overlooking the old Harwich Quay. In preparation for the introduction of the new* **Stena Hollandica** *and 'Britannica' in 2010 the linkspan was converted for two level loading and the lifting portal was replaced by lifting towers. In the background the original two linkspans are visible. One of these was destroyed in November 1989 when a dredger ran into it during dense fog while the other one was demolished later. (John Hendy)*

Above: Following the end of the Second World War the railway system in Britain was nationalised by the Government. The British Transport Company with British Rail expanded the train ferry service from Harwich to Zeebrugge. The **Norfolk Ferry**, **Suffolk Ferry**, **Essex Ferry**, and later the **Cambridge Ferry** were to become regular daily visitors to the River Stour. The **Essex Ferry** is seen here leaving the Hook of Holland for Harwich with trade cars. (John Hendy)

Middle left: British Rail built their last traditional classic passenger ferry, the **Avalon**, which was built to maintain the Harwich-Hook of Holland route and also to embark on their cruise programme to various parts of Europe, including the Baltic and the Canary Islands. The **Avalon** is seen at Swan Hunters yard in 1975, undergoing her conversion to a car ferry. (Ferry Publications Library)

Below: An aerial view of Parkeston Quay showing the **Prinz Oberon** and Sealink's **St. Nicholas** loading for her morning sailing to the Hook of Holland. (FotoFlite)

Left: *To enable the* **Stena Britannica** *to berth at Parkeston Quay major modifications had to be undertaken at the port, including the provision of a new linkspan. This view shows the 'Britannica' at the port unloading freight. (Ferry Publications Library)*

Below: *The* **Stena Britannica** *(2000) leaves the berth at Parkeston Quay for the Hook of Holland. (FotoFlite)*

Harwich
Hook of Holland
1893-2020

PRINCIPAL VESSELS USED ON THE HARWICH-HOOK ROUTE 1893-1993.

Stoomvaart Maatschappij Zeeland
Koninklijke Nederlandsche Postvaart N. V.

* not used between Hook of Holland and Harwich.

		built	in service
1 *	ps Stad Middelburg	1865	1875 – 1888
2 *	ps Stad Vlissingen	1865	1875 – 1879
3 *	ps Stad Breda	1863	1875 – 1883
4 *	ps Prinses Elisabeth	1878	1878 – 1898
5 *	ps Prinses Marie	1878	1878 – 1898
6 *	ps Prins Hendrik	1880	1880 – 1902
7 *	ps Willem, Prins van Oranje	1883	1883 – 1909
8 *	ps Duitschland	1886	1886 – 1922
9 *	ps Engeland	1886	1886 – 1911
10 *	ps Nederland	1887	1887 – 1910
11 *	ps Koningin Wilhelmina (I)	1895	1895 – 1916
12 *	ps Koningin Regentes	1895	1895 – 1918
13 *	ps Prins Hendrik (2)	1895	1895 – 1922
14 *	ss Prinses Juliana (1)	1909	1909 – 1916
15	ss Oranje Nassau	1909	1909 – 1954
16 *	ss Mecklenburg (1)	1909	1909 – 1916
17	ss Prinses Juliana (2)	1920	1920 – 1940
18	ss Mecklenburg (2)	1922	1922 – 1960
19	ms Koningin Emma	1939	1939 – 1968
20	ms Prinses Beatrix (1)	1939	1939 – 1968
21	ms Koningin Wilhelmina (2)	1960	1960 – 1978
22	ms Koningin Juliana	1968	1968 – 1984
23	ms Prinses Beatrix (2)	1978	1978 – 1985
24	ms Koningin Beatrix	1986	1986 – 1989

On bare boat-harter to S.M.Zeeland:

		built	in service
31	ms Zeeland	1973	1984 – 1986

Stena Line B. V., Hook of Holland

		built	in service
61	ms Koningin Beatrix	1986	1989 –1989

On bare boat-harter to Stena Line B.V.:

		built	in service
41	ms Stena Seatrader	1973	1990 – 2008

On time charter to Stena Line B. V.:

		built	in service
51	ms Stena Normandy	1981	1991
52	ms Stena Britannica	1981	1991 –1994
53	ms Stena Traveller	1992	1992

SERVICE: HARWICH – Hook of Holland
ROTTERDAM ANTWERP
ZEEBRUGGE

Great Eastern Railway Company
London & North Eastern Railway
British Transport Commission
British Railways/British Rail
Sealink (UK) Ltd
Sealink Stena Line Ltd
Stena Sealink Ltd

		built	in service
101	ps Avalon (1)	1864	1864 – 1866
102	ps Zealous	1864	1864 – 1887
103	ps Harwich	1864	1864 – 1907
104	ps Rotterdam	1864	1864 – 1887
a	ss Peterboro	1864	1887 – 1908
105	ps Avalon (2)	1865	1865 – 1888
106	ps Ravensbury	1865	1865 – 1870
107	ps Great Yarmouth	1866	1866 – 1871
108	ps Richard Young	1871	1871 – 1890
a	ss Brandon	1871	1890 – 1905
109	ps Pacific	1864	1872 – 1887
110	ps Claud Hamilton	1875	1875 – 1897
111	ps Princess of Wales	1878	1878 – 1896
112	ps Lady Tyler	1880	1880 – 1893
113	ps Adelaide	1880	1880 – 1896
114	ss Norwich	1883	1883 – 1905
115	ss Ipswich	1883	1883 – 1907
116	ss Cambridge	1887	1887 – 1912
117	ss Colchester (1)	1889	1889 – 1918
118	ss Chelmsford	1893	1893 – 1910
119	ss Berlin	1894	1894 – 1907
120	ss Amsterdam (1)	1894	1894 – 1928
121	ss Vienna (1)	1894	1894 – 1920
a	ss Roulers	1894	1920 – 1930
122	ss Dresden	1897	1897 – 1915
a	ss HMS Louvain	1897	1915 – 1918
123	ss Cromer	1902	1902 – 1934
124	ss Brussels	1902	1902 – 1917 /1918 –
1920			
125	ss Yarmouth	1903	1903 – 1908
126	ss Clacton	1904	1904 – 1917
127	ss Newmarket	1907	1907 – 1918
128	ts Copenhagen	1907	1907 – 1917
129	ts Munich	1908	1908 – 1916
a	ts St. Denis	1908	1916 – 1940
130	ts St. Petersburg	1910	1910 – 1916
a	ts Archangel	1910	1916 – 1941
131	ts Stockholm	1917	– (requisitioned on stocks)
132	ss Felixstowe	1918	1918 – 1941 /1946 –
1948			
133	ss Kilkenny	1903	1917 – 1919
a	ss Frinton	1903	1919 – 1929
134	ts St. George (1)	1906	1919 – 1929
135	ts Antwerp	1920	1920 – 1950
136	ts Bruges	1920	1920 – 1940
137	ts Malines	1922	1922 – 1942
138	ss Sheringham	1926	1926 – 1958
139	ts Vienna (2)	1929	1929 – 1960
140	ts Prague	1930	1930 – 1948
141	ts Amsterdam (2)	1930	1930 – 1944
142	ss Dewsbury	1910	1918 – 1919 /1946 –
1959			
143	ss Accrington	1910	1918 – 1919 /1946-1951
144	ss Arnhem	1947	1947 – 1968

145	ss Duke of York	1935	1948 – 1963
146	ss Amsterdam (3)	1950	1950 – 1968
147	ms Isle of Ely	1958	1958 – 1969 /1969 – 1975
148	ms Colchester (2)	1959	1959 – 1973 /1973 – 1975
149	ss Avalon (3)	1963	1963 – 1974 /1974 – 1981
150	ms Seafreightliner I	1967	1967 – 1986 /laid up – 87
151	ms Seafreightliner II	1967	1967 – 1986 /laid up – 87
152	ms St. George (2)	1968	1968 – 1983 /laid up – 84
153	ms St. Edmund	1974	1974 – 1982 /requisitioned by MOD
154	ms St. Nicholas	1981	1983 – 1991

Bare-boat charters

| 51 | ms Stena Normandy | 1981 | 1991* |
| 52 | ms Stena Britannica | 1981 | 1991 –1994 |

* This ship is now based on the Southampton – Cherbourg route.

THE SHIPS OF THE ROUTES

Abbreviations:
4sa = 4 stroke single acting / m = metres / hp = horse power (0,736 x = kW) / B.A.O.R. = British Army on Rhine.

THE DUTCH FLEET

Ships of the S.M.Z., in relation with the route.
Issue: 29-03-1993.

15 ORANJE NASSAU

Gross tonnage	3053	Nett tonnage	1121
Deadweight	2405		
Dimensions	110,64m x 13,50m x 7,24m;		
Engine	twin screw steamer built by Fairfield Shipbuilding & Engineering Co. Ltd., Glasgow, 2 x T3cyl; 10000 hp; 22 knots		
Capacity	246 1st class / 110 2nd class passengers		
Ordered	16-11-1908		
Launched	05-07-1909		
Builder	Fairfield Shipbuilding & Engineering Co. Ltd., Glasgow (462).		
Entered service	11-1909		
Route	Flushing and Queenborough, 1911 Folkestone, 1927 Harwich, 1946 Hook-Harwich		

06-1911 visited the "fleet-review" at Spithead; 01-01-1927 arrived as the first ship of S.M.Z. on the route Flushing-Harwich at Parkeston Quay; summer 1928 hotelship in Amsterdam during the Olympic Games; 11-05-1940 sailed from Flushing to the Downs, later to London and in management of Wm.H.Muller &

Co (London) Ltd.; 29-08-1941 in use in Holyhead as accommodation ship of the Royal Netherlands Navy 27-08-1945 until 29-06-1946 in service as a trooper between London/Harwich and Rotterdam; 29-07-1946 back in civilian service between Hook of Holland and Harwich; between 1949 and 1952 every summer in charter of Batavier Line Rotterdam-London v.v.; relief ship until she left for the last voyage to the breakers yard. 12-07-1954 arrived at Hendrik Ido Ambacht (Holland) for breaking up by N.V. Holland Scrapyard.

17 PRINSES JULIANA (2)

Gross tonnage	2908	Nett tonnage	1122
Deadweight	2407	Draft	4,27m
Dimensions	110,72m x 13,01 m		
Engine	Kon. Mij De Schelde, Vlissingen, 2 x T3cyl; 10000 hp; 22 knots		
Capacity	267 1st class / 110 2nd class passengers		
Ordered	22-05-1917	Keel laid	27-11-1917
Launched	13-03-1920		
Builder	Koninklijke Maatschappij De Schelde, Vlissingen (=Flushing) (171).		
Entered service	12-08-1920		
Route	Flushing-Folkestone; used several times on service to the Hook		

11-05-1940 requisitioned by the Dutch Navy; 12-05-1940 attacked by German aircraft near the entrance of Hook of Holland, during the voyage from Flushing to IJmuiden with troops and military horses. Heavily damaged, grounded north of north pier of Hook of Holland. All troops and crew were saved, one crew member died during the attack. Broke in two on 24-06-1940. The remains of the wreck are still in the same position.

18 MECKLENBURG (2)

Gross tonnage	2907	Nett tonnage	1122
Deadweight	2408	Draft	4,27m
Dimensions	110,72m x 13,01 m		
Engine	twin screw steamer built by Fairfield Shipbuilding & Engineering Co. Ltd., Glasgow, 2 x T3cyl; 10000 hp; 22 knots		
Capacity	246 1st class / 110 2nd class passengers		
Ordered	22-11-1916	Keel laid	04-02-1919
Launched	18-03-1922		
Builder	Koninklijke Maatschappij De Schelde, Vlissingen (170).		
Entered service	19-07-1922		
Route	Flushing-Folkestone/Hook-Harwich		
Maiden voyage	23-07-1922		
04-09-1939	laid up in Flushing		

11-05-1940 sailed via the Downs to London and laid up there. In management of Wm. H. Müller & Co (London) Ltd in use as military accommodation ship in Portsmouth between 09-10-1940 and 15-01-1941; depot ship for NAAFI, later submarine service until 30-05-1943. Requisitioned by the Royal Navy and converted as landing ship for the Infantry, took part in the landings on the coast of Normandy in 06-1944 21-11-1945 until 04-04-1946 in use as trooper between Rotterdam and London and Harwich; 16-04-1946 back in civilian service; 1947 refitted and changed to oil burning boilers by Wilton Fijenoord, Schiedam (Holland); capacity 67 1st cl pass/ 450 deck pass.; 13-06-1947 maiden voyage from Rotterdam to Harwich with invited persons and 14-06-1947 first trip with passengers on the Hook of Holland-Harwich route; in the summers of 1949 until 1952 on the Flushing-Folkestone route, but that was not successful; 25-10-1959 laid up; 15-05-1960 arrived in Gent (Belgium) for breaking up by Van Heijghen Freres.

19 KONINGIN EMMA

Gross tonnage	4353	Nett tonnage	2188
Deadweight	2994	Draft	4,40m
Dimensions	115,82m x 14,38m		
Engine	twin screw motorship built by De Schelde/Sulzer, 2 x 10cyl 2sa diesels; 12500 hp; 23 knots		
Capacity	297 night service/1800 day service; 35 cars.		
Ordered	12-1937	Keel laid	07-05-1938
Launched	14-01-1939		
Builder	Koninklijke Maatschappij De Schelde, Vlissingen (209); sea trials 19-05-1939.		
Entered service	06-1939		
Route	Flushing-Harwich/Hook-Harwich		
Maiden voyage	04-06-1939		
02-09-1939	laid up in Flushing		

10-05-1940 sailed via the Downs to London; 17-05-1940 in service of Ministry of War Transports; After 09-1940 converted by Harland & Wolff, Belfast as landing ship; entered service 14-01-1941 as HMS *Queen Emma* and used all over the world. 29-04-1946 returned to Flushing, converted as ferry in civilian service with a capacity of 1423 pass in day service or 203 1st cl pass/ 94 2nd cl pass; 28-02-1948 sea trials; 05-03-1948 maiden voyage Hook of Holland-Harwich in the night service in charter of B.R.; summer 1948 in charter of Batavier Line Rotterdam-London; 18-12-1968 towed to Antwerp and broken up by Jos de Smedt.

20 PRINSES BEATRIX (1)

Gross tonnage	4353	Nett tonnage	2188
Deadweight	2994	Draft	4,40m
Dimensions	115,82m x 14,38m		
Engine	as detailed nr 19		
Capacity	297 night service/1800 day service; 35 cars.		
Ordered	12-1937	Keel laid	07-05-1938
Launched	25-03-1939		
Builder	Koninklijke Maatschappij De Schelde, Vlissingen (210); sea trials 24-06-1939.		
Entered service	07-1939		
Route	Flushing-Harwich/Hook-Harwich		
Maiden voyage	03-07-1939		
02-09-1939	laid up in Flushing		

10-05-1940 as detailed nr 19; 22-01-1941 renamed HMS *Princess Beatrix*
13-04-1946 returned to Flushing and converted to a civilian ferry; 07/08-09-1946 on charter to Dutch Government in service between Rotterdam-Harwich; 29-05-1948 sea trials; 31-05-1948 maiden voyage Hook of Holland-Harwich; 09-1968 laid up in Schiedam; 19-12-1968 towed to Antwerp for breaking up by Jos de Smedt.

21 KONINGIN WILHELMINA

Gross tonnage	6228	Nett tonnage	2727
Deadweight	732	Draft	4,89m
Dimensions	120,02m x 17,33m		
Engine	twin screw motorship built M.A.N., Augsburg		
	(Germany), 2 x 12cyl 2sa diesels; 15600 hp; 21 knots		
Capacity	1600 passengers day service or 100 night service; 60 cars.		
Ordered	06-1956		
Launched	30-05-1959		
Builder	N.V. Scheepswerf & Machinefabriek "De Merwede", Hardinxveld (548); 8 + 11-01-1960 sea trials.		
Entered service	30-01-1960		
Route	Hook of Holland-Harwich		
Maiden voyage	07-02-1960		

15-06-1967 Queen Juliana opened from this ship the new entrance of IJmuiden and on 11-06-1971 the opening of the new entrance to Europoort by Queen Juliana. 01-07-1978 laid up in Flushing as relief ship; 10-12-1978 sailed Flushing as *Captain Constantinos* and arrived in Piraeus 18-12-1978; refitted and converted as ro/ro passenger ferry; owned by C. Ventouris & Sons, Piraeus and came in service between Syros-Tinos-Mykonos and Piraeus; 1981 - Renamed *Panagia Tinoy* In 1987 she was sold to AK Ventouris and transferred in 1990 to Ventouris Sea Lines when she was renamed *Artemis* and used for day cruising. Sold at auction in 1996 to Minoan Cruises for cruises from Heraklion - Rethymnon - Agios Nikolaos and Santorini. On 30 April 2001 sold to Vickie Navigation, Honduras for scrapping and renamed *Temis*. 14 May 2001 arrived at Alang, India for breaking up.

22 KONINGIN JULIANA

Gross tonnage	6682	Nett tonnage	3475
Deadweight	1290	Draft	5,10m
Dimensions	131,02m x 20,48m		
Engine	built by M.A.N. Augsburg (Germany), 4 x 9cyl 4sa diesels; 19200 hp; 21 knots		
Capacity	1200 passengers day service or 750 night service; 220 cars.		
Keel laid	04-1967	Sea trials	07/08-09-1968
Launched	02-02-1968		
Builder	Cammell Laird &: Co. Ltd., Birkenhead (England) (1331); 13-06-1968 suffered from fire during construction.		
Entered service	14-10-1968		
Route	Hook of Holland-Harwich (she was first S.M.Z. ro/ro passenger ferry)		
Maiden voyage	17-10-1968		

08-04-1984 laid up in Rotterdam; 24-12-1984 sold to Mr. Tromp, Leiden (Holland) and repainted with red, white and blue hull as *Holland Trade Ship*; 06-02-1985 left Rotterdam for Amsterdam and laid up again under her original name, owned by Administratie-en bemiddelingskantoor Tromp, Kampen (Holland); 09-1985 sold to Navigazione Arcipelago Maddalenino SpA, Naples; 10-10-1985 sailed from Amsterdam after renaming as *Moby Prince* and in use as ferry between Naples and Cagliari. 11-04-1991 collided with the anchored Italian tanker *Agip Abbruzzio*, off the Italian coast near Leghorn. The *Moby Prince* was completely gutted by fire and 141 persons died and only 1 survived. The gutted wreck laid up in Leghorn. In June 1998 the wreck was salvaged by Smit Tak BV and towed to Aliga in Turkey where she arrived 22 July 1998 for scrapping.

23 PRINSES BEATRIX (2)

Gross tonnage	9356	Nett tonnage	4862
Deadweight	1887	Draft	5,17m
Dimensions	132,16m x 22,56m		
Engine	twin screw motorship built by Stork Werkspoor, 4 x 8cyl 4sa diesels, 22000 hp; 21 knots		
Capacity	1500 passengers day service /966 passengers night service; 320 cars		
Sea trials	05-1978		
Launched	14-01-1978		
Builder	Schweepswerf Verolme, Heusden (959)		
Entered service	24-06-1978		
Route	Hook of Holland-Harwich		
Maiden voyage	29-06-1978		

01-10-1985 sold to Brittany Ferries and came under French flag, port of registry: Caen, but chartered back by S.M.Z. for use on the route; Dutch crew remained on board with an extra French captain; 01-05-1986 delivered to Brittany Ferries in Rotterdam and renamed *Duc de Normandie*, refitted in Rotterdam for the Caen-Portsmouth service (Societe Economique Mixte d'Armement Naval du Calvados); 05-06-1986 maiden voyage Portsmouth-Caen. Left Brittany Ferries on 30 September 2004 and put up for sale. She was laid up in Gdansk, Poland from 15 November 2004 and in March 2005 was sold to Trans Europe Ferries, Limassol and renamed *Wisteria*. She was then refitted in Ostend and chartered to Ferrimaroc for service between Almeria - Nador until October 2005. She briefly sailed between Ostend - Ramsgate in November 2005 and was then chartered in January 2006 to Acciona Trasmediterranea / Ferrimaroc, Spain for further service between Almeria - Nador. Sold in 2013 to Nizhniy Shipping Ltd., Slovenia, and re-named *Vronsky*. Still in service: Algeciras to Tanger Med (Mediterranean)

24 KONINGIN BEATRIX

Gross tonnage	31189	Nett tonnage	15170
Deadweight	3060	Draft	6,20m
Dimensions	161,78m x 27,60m		
Engine	twin screw motorship built by M.A.N. Augsburg (Germany) 4 x 8cyl 4sa diesels; 26000 hp; 21 knots		
Capacity	2100 passengers day service/1879 night service (1991 reduced to 1800 day/ night); 500 cars.		
Keel laid	25-01-1985	Sea trials	11/14-03-1986
Launched	09-11-1985		
Builder	Van der Giessen De Noord, Krimpen aan de IJssel (935).		
Entered service	16-04-1986		
Route	Hook of Holland-Harwich		
Maiden voyage	22-04-1986		

01-1989 repainted with Crown Line logo in the side; 01-09-1989 delivered in the company take-over to Stena Line BV and repainted in Stena livery. Her last day of service was 2 June 1997. On 19 June 1997 she was re-registered in London for service with Stena Line UK between Fishguard - Rosslare where she remained on that route until 12 March 2002.Renamed *Stena Baltica* on 13 March 2002 and put into service between Karlskrona and Gdynia. From February 2005 until 5 June 2005 she was rebuilt at Remontowa, Gdansk and then returned to the same route where she remained until being displaced by the former Harwich - Hook vessel *Stena Hollandica* or *Stena Britannica*.

BAREBOAT CHARTERS

31 ZEELAND

Gross tonnage	6801	Nett tonnage	3370
Deadweight	1202	Draft	5,50m
Dimensions	128,12m x 19,99m		
Engine	twin screw motorship built by Werkspoor, 4 x 8cyl 4sa diesels, 20400 hp; 23 knots		
Capacity	634 passengers in berths and 866 on deck, total 1500 passengers		
Launched	1972		
Builder	Ateliers & Chanriers du Havre, Graville, France (212) as *Peter Wessel* for A/S Larvik Frederikshavnferjen (Larvik Line), Larvik, Norway for service between Larvik and Frederikshavn.		
Entered service	26-07-1973		

03-1984 chartered out for 2 years to Stoomvaart Maatschappij Zeeland, Hook of Holland for service between Hook of Holland and Harwich. Registration under Bahamian flag and owned by Admiralty Shipping Co. Nassau, Bahamas. Repainted and renamed to *Zeeland* at Larvik, 01-04-1984 she entered service from the Hook. 04-1986 delivered back to A/S Larvik Frederikshavnferjen in Rotterdam. Sold by LF to Stena Line A/B and delivered to Rotterdam, renamed *Stena Nordica*. 23-11-1988 sold to Jadrolinija, Yugoslavia and left Gothenburg the next day as *Marko Polo* for the Adriatic Sea. 10 January 1992 - Chartered to TT-Line for service with TR Line between Trelleborg - Rostock. In 1993 was chartered to Olympic Ferries and put into service between Bari - Igoumenitsa - Patras whilst between May and September 1994 she was chartered to Compagnie Marocaine de Navigation for the route Nador - Sete. 1995 saw her returned to Jadrolinija Cruises between Ancona and Split. Since then has spent the majority of her time in the Adriatic, variously between Rijeka-Split-Dubrovnik and Bari. Still in service. Still in service: as *Marko Polo* with Jadrolinija - Ancona to Gazenica (Adriatic)

STENA LINE BV (OWNER)

61 KONINGIN BEATRIX

(see details nr 24)

BAREBOAT CHARTER STENA LINE BV

41 STENA SEATRADER

Gross tonnage	5160	Nett tonnage	1598
Deadweight	2985	Draft	5,54m
Dimensions	148,01m x 22,13m		
Engine	Lindholmens Motor Akt, Gothenburg, 2 x 6cyl 4sa diesels + 2 x 8cyl 4sa diesels; 14000 hp; 18,5 knots		
Capacity	36 passengers		
Builder	A/S Nakskov Shipyard, Nakskov, Denmark (199) for Lion Ferry A/B, Halmstad, Sweden and chartered out to the Swedish State Railways (SJ), named *Svealand*, in service between Trelleborg and Sassnitz.		
Entered service	09-1973		

1981 charter finished. 1982 sold to Rederi A/B Nordo, Maimo, Sweden and lengthened by 33m to 181,60m length overall and new draft 6,22m by Howaldtswerke/Deutsche Werft AG, Hamburg, new section (507); renamed *Svealand av Malmö*; Gross tonnage 6962,41; Nett tonnage 2874,85; Deadweight 6130. Re-engined: Pielstick 2x2 8cyl 4sa diesels of 4000 hp each and Pielstick 2x2 6cyl 4sa diesels of 3000 hp each. 11-1982 entered service between Malmö and Travemünde.

1987 major rebuilding was carried out by Wartsila Marine Industries Inc., Turku Shipyard, Finland, in which the accommodation was lifted and extended, including a new part of cargospaces were fitted under the accommodation. Renamed *Svea Link*.

1989 sold to Stena A/B, Gothenburg, Sweden and resold to Lily Shipping BV, Amsterdam (100% subsidiary of Stena International BV, Amsterdam)

04-1990 chartered out by Lily Shipping BV to Stena Line BV, Hook of Holland for 5 years and renamed *Stena Seatrader*. Gross tonnage 6962; Nett tonnage 2874; Deadweight 6130; Port of registry: Hook of Holland.

01-05-1990 entered service between Hook of Holland and Harwich as a freight vessel with accommodation for 223 passengers and 29 crew. From 2 May 1990 was in service on the Harwich - Hook route until being transferred to the Hook - Killingholme route in March 2001. 12 August 2006 saw her leave that route for service in the Irish Sea. She was refitted at Birkenhead in August 2006 before joining the Holyhead - Dublin route on 9 October 2006. She remained there until 12 November 2008 after which she left for lay up and sale in Rotterdam. In December 2008 she was chartered to Ventouris Group and renamed *Seatrade*. February 2009 - in service between Igoumenitsa - Bari.

TIME CHARTERS STENA LINE BV

51 STENA NORMANDY
(see details Harwich-fleet nr 154)

52 STENA BRITANNICA
(see details Harwich-fleet nr 52)

53 STENA TRAVELLER

Gross tonnage	18625	Nett tonnage	5585	
Deadweight	4,27m	Draft	5275	
Dimensions	110,72 m x 13,01m			
Engine	twin screw motorship built by Sulzer/Wartsila; 2 x 8cyl diesels; 14400 hp; 18 knots			
Capacity	capacity 141 pass. (accommodation was not furnished completely)			
Launched	01-1992			
Builder	Fosen Mek. Verksteder A/S, Rissa, Norway (51).			

Delivered to Stena Rederi AB, Gothenburg, Sweden and laid up in Norway. Maiden voyage from Norway to Hook of Holland to temporarily replace the *Stena Seatrader*, which was due to be chartered out for 10 weeks to the Mediterranean, but was cancelled at the last moment. *Stena Traveller* arrived in Hook of Holland on 28-02-1992. *Stena Traveller* had only two weeks to replace *Stena Seatrader* during drydocking, between Hook of Holland and Harwich and left the Hook for Southampton on 14-04-1992. She took a new charter for Sealink Stena Line Ltd for 6 months, between Southampton and Cherbourg. After she was chartered by TT Line in the Baltic. Renamed *TT Traveller*. Still in service.

THE HARWICH FLEET

101 AVALON

Gross tonnage	613
Dimensions	70,15m x 8,26m
Engine	paddle steamer; 12 knots
Launched	1864
Builder	Messrs J & W Dudgeon of Poplar (London)
Entered service	13-06-1864
Route	Harwich-Rotterdam

1866 sold to the Government of Brazil.

102 ZEALOUS

Gross tonnage	613	Nett tonnage	455
Deadweight	499	Draft	3,56m
Dimensions	70,15m x 8,24m		
Engine	paddle steamer, J & W Dudgeon: oscil. 2cyl 54"-30"; 220 NHP (1060 pk); 10 knots		
Launched	24-05-1864 by Miss. Goodson		
Builder	Messrs J & W Dudgeon of Poplar (London)		
Entered service	01-08-1864		
Route	Harwich-Rotterdam		

1873 rebuilt for trading passengers/freight and reboilered.
1887 sold for scrap.

103 HARWICH (master Mr Elwaid)

Gross tonnage	750	Nett tonnage	550
Deadweight	613	Draft	4,27m
Dimensions	65,58m x 8,24m		
Engine	paddle steamer, details not known; (1060 pk); 10 knots.		
Launched	13-08-1864 Entered service 1864		
Builder	Messrs Simpson of London.		

1884 rebuilt as twin screw steamer, reboilered by Earle's Co., Hull.; engine comp. 4cyl, 153 NHP, Earle's Co., Hull.
1889 converted to a cattle-carrier, 05-03-1889 delivered as the first cattle-ship on the Harwich-Rotterdam route.
Lloyds register 1899

Gross tonnage 778 Nett tonnage			380.

10-1907 sold for scrap to Holland.

104 ROTTERDAM (master Mr Howison)

Gross tonnage	757	Nett tonnage	557
Draft	4,27m		
Dimensions	65,58m x 8,24m		
Engine	paddle steamer, oscil 2cyl 5 5"-66", 220 NHP (1060 pk); 10 knots. ___		
Launched	1864	Entered service 1864	
Builder	Messrs Simpson of London. Anchors and chains proved at a public machine (Lloyds Register 1865).		

1887 rebuilt as twin screw steamer; engine: Earle's Co. comp. 4cyl, 168 NHP; reboilered by Earle's Co. of Hull and converted to a cattle-carrier.
1887 renamed *Peterboro*; Lloyds Register 1899:

Gross tonnage	847	Nett tonnage	427
Deadweight	749		

1908 sold for scrap.

105 AVALON

Gross tonnage	670	Nett tonnage	478
Deadweight	571	Draft	4,27m
Dimensions	73,10m x 8,24m		

Engine	paddle steamer built by J & W Dudgeon; oscil 2 cyl, 54"-54", 220 NHP (1060 pk); 14 knots
Launched	03-06-1864 Entered service 1865
Builder	Messrs J & W Dudgeon of Poplar (London).

1876 new engines and boilers. 1888 sold to Earle's Co., Hull and not renamed. 1890 rebuilt as screw steamer by Earle's Co., Hull.

Lloyds Register 1909

Gross tonnage	843	Nett tonnage	507
Engine	Earle's Co, Hull, T3cyl 18", 27"& 46"-33". Before 1906 sold to T. Rasmussen, Norway, port of registry: Stavanger.		

1909 wrecked on the coast of Jamaica.

106 RAVENSBURY (master R. Elward)

Gross tonnage	621
Dimensions	73,12m x 8,24m x 4,09m
Engine	paddle steamer, oscil. compound 2cyl 54"-54", 220 NHP (=1000 ipk); 14 knots; draught 2,75m.
Builder	Messrs J & W Dudgeon of Poplar (London).

Entered service in 1865

22-12-1868 grounded near Slijkgat (Goeree) and refloated the next day; 05-01-1869 grounded again, outward bound from Rotterdam at high water at Schulpenplaat, next day refloated by herself. The third time was to be the last.

05-03-1870 sailed from Harwich, bound for Rotterdam and later that day grounded again at Schulpenplaat. Passengers disembarked. 06-03-1870 little moving of the ship but not refloated. 07-03-1870 the boiler fires were extinguished and three tugs with a barge arrived at the wreck to salvage the cargo and mail. 08-03-1870 the crew abandoned the ship. 09-03-1870 the tugs with barge, cargo and mail arrived at Den Briel and later Rotterdam. The ship broke into two pieces.

1971 (after 101 years) during dredging works at Maasvlakte, the wreck was found in the Hartelkanaal. The forepart was lifted and scrapped, but parts of the engines are still (1992) on the banks of Hartelkanaal and a part of the stern still remains in the canal bank.

107 GREAT YARMOUTH (master Mr Tyier)

Gross tonnage	731	Nett tonnage	491
Dimensions	60,92m x 8,64m x 5,19m		
Engine	single screw steamer built by R & W Hawthorn, Newcastle; comp. inverted, 2cyl, 25" & 48"-30" 100 NHP; 10 knots		
Launched	06-1866 Entered service 1866		
Builder	Jones Bros., London.		

She had not enough accommodation for passengers. 1872 sold to T.G. Beatley, London/Harwich, not renamed. 1880 sold to R.B. Fenwick & J Reay, Harwich/Newcastle. 1881 grounded in the Gulf of Bothnia and later refloated. 09/1887 wrecked and total loss.

108 RICHARD YOUNG (master G. Rivers)

Gross tonnage	718	Nett tonnage	405
Deadweight	571		
Dimensions	73,1Om x 8,24m x 4,09m		
Engine	paddle steamer built by J & W Dudgeon, London, oscil 2cyl 54"-54" 950 pk; 14 knots.		
Launched	1871 Entered service 03-1872		
Builder	Messrs J & W Dudgeon of Poplar (London).		

Became famous as the first sea-going ship which passed through the New Rotterdam Waterway at the Hook of Holland on her maiden voyage. 03-1889 converted into a cattle-carrier.

1890 converted to screw steamer and reboilered by Earle's Co., Hull and after that renamed *Brandon*.

Lloyds Register 1899

Gross tonnage	668	Nett tonnage	305
Deadweight	582		
Engine	Earle's Co., Hull, T3cyl 20½", 32" & 54"-33", 168 NHP.		

1905 sold for scrap.

109 PACIFIC

Gross tonnage	712	Nett tonnage	515
Deadweight	507		
Dimensions	71,80m x 8,08m x 3,48m		
Engine	paddle steamer built by C. Lungley, London, oscil. 2cyl 48"-54", 170 NHP; 10 knots.		
Launched	1864		
Builder	C. Lungley, Deptford, London for unspecified owners, (before 1872 not mentioned in LR).		

1872 bought by the Great Eastern Railway Co. and kept original name. This ship was cheaper in use than the *Avalon* and *Ravensbury*, used 20 tons of coal less per week and 2 seafarers less on board.

1887 sold for scrap.

110 CLAUD HAMILTON (master G. Rivers-1880)

Gross tonnage	962	Nett tonnage	565
Deadweight	677		
Dimensions	76,71m x 9,20m x 4,14m		
Engine	paddle steamer built by J. Elder & Co., Glasgow, first compound/oscil. type of G.E.R., 2cyl 54" & 95"-63", 350 NHP (2000 ipk); 14 knots		
Launched	03-06-1875		
Builder	John Elder & Co. Govan, Glasgow (187) (to be the first ship for G.E.R. built on the Clyde).		
Maiden voyage	14-08-1875		

The biggest ship of the company, named after the Chairman of G.E.R. She was the last paddle steamer of the G.E.R.-fleet. 1897 sold to the Corporation of the City of London and not renamed. Used between Gravesend and Deptford on the Thames as cattle-carrier. (LR 1905: b 972; master G. Harris).

07-1914 sold for scrap to Holland.

111 PRINCESS OF WALES (master G. Rivers)

Gross tonnage	1098	Nett tonnage	648
Deadweight	798		
Dimensions	80,95m x 9,25m x 4,32m		
Engine	paddle steamer built by London & Glasgow Co., Glasgow, simple oscil 2cyl, cyl length 68", stroke 84"; 2500 ipk; 15 knots		
Capacity	580 passengers		
Launched	02-02-1878		
Builder	London & Glasgow Eng. & Shipbuilding Co., Govan (Clyde). 3 masts.		
Maiden voyage	06-07-1878		

1894 replaced by ss *Berlin*. 16-05-1895 sold for scrap.

112 LADY TYLER (master W.S. Gray)

Gross tonnage	951	Nett tonnage	421
Deadweight	802		
Dimensions	79,61m x 9,20m x 4,17m		
Engine	paddle steamer built by R & W Hawthorn & Co, Newcastle, compound 6cyl (4 hp and 2 Ip cyl) (2) 33" & (4) 44"-60"; 1400 hp; 13 knots		
Capacity	700 passengers and fitted with electric light		
Sea trials	04-05-1880		
Builder	Messrs T & W Smith, North Shields.		
Maiden voyage	29-05-1880		

1893 sold to Earle's Shipyards Co., Hull and replaced by the *Chelmsford*. 1895 chartered to Mutual Line of Manx Steamers as competitors of the Isle of Man Steam Packet Co.
1897 renamed *Artemis* and remained as property of Earle's Co., Hull, (LR 1898: b 1010; n 558; d 568. 1900 in use as a coal-hulk at Gravesend and renamed *George Sandford*, unspecified owners. Remained there till 1955! after which she was sold for scrap.

113 ADELAIDE (master H. Shedlock)

Gross tonnage	927	Nett tonnage	441
Deadweight	757		
Dimensions	79,30m x 9,84m x 3,97m		
Engine	paddle steamer built by Barrow Shipbuilding Co. Ltd., Barrow, comp. oscil. 2cyl 45" & 87"-72"; 1600 hp; 14½ knots		
Capacity	682 passengers		
Launched	08-05-1880 by Mrs. Simpson, wife of one of the directors		
Builder	Barrow Shipbuilding Co. Ltd., Barrow.		
Maiden voyage	23-07-1880		

This ship was the first completely built from steel and was the last driven by paddles, designed for the Continental services. 1896 sold to T.W. Ward and in 1897 sold again to J. Bannatyne & Sons for scrap. Replaced by *ss Amsterdam*.

114 NORWICH (master J.T. Henderson)

Gross tonnage	1037	Nett tonnage	437
Deadweight	816		
Dimensions	79,30m x 9,53m x 4,58m		
Engine	twin screw steamer built by Earle's Co., Hull, 2 sets of inverted diagonal compound machinery 2cyl 30" & 57"-36"; 2 boilers, 80 Ib/inch²; 14½ knots.		
Capacity	84 1st class / 42 2nd class passengers		
Launched	06-03-1883		
Builder	Earle's Shipbuilding & Engineering Co. (Ltd). Hull, formerly C&W Earle, (255)		
Maiden voyage	24-07-1883 (under Captain Nickerson)		

1897 new boilers placed. 1905 sold to Queenstown Dry Docks Sb. & E. Co. Ltd, port of registry: Harwich
Lloyds Register 1908

Gross tonnage 1352		Nett tonnage	707
Deadweight	707		

1911 sold to J. DOS Santos Silva, Ilha do Fogo, Cape Verde Islands and renamed *Fortuna*. 1913 sold again to Continental Trading Co., New York, USA and renamed *Evelyn* for services from Montevideo to USA. 1915 sold to Cuneo Importing Co. Inc., New York, USA and renamed *Neptune*. 03-1921 sank.

115 IPSWICH (master J.H. Robinson) (sistership of Norwich)

Gross tonnage	1037	Nett tonnage	435
Deadweight	820		
Dimensions	79,30m x 9,53m x 4,58m		
Engine	twin screw steamer for further details see nr 114 *Norwich*		
Launched	21-05-1883		
Builder	Earle's S&E Co., Hull (256).		
Maiden voyage	23-10-1883		

1895 new boilers placed. 1905 sold to Joseph Constant, London, port of registry: Harwich; for services in British India. Lloyds Register 1908: sold to Shah Steam Navigation Co. of India Ltd, Harwich and still with the same name.
05-1909 sold for scrap.

116 CAMBRIDGE (master R.A. Henderson)

Gross tonnage	1160	Nett tonnage	519
Deadweight	906		
Dimensions	85,53m x 9,46m x 4,63m		
Engine	twin screw steamer built by Earle's Co., Hull, comp. 2x2cyl 30" & 57"-36"; 14½ knots		
Capacity	730 passengers		
Launched	11-10-1886		
Builder	Earle's S&E Co., Hull (299)		
Maiden voyage	12-02-1887		
Route	Harwich-Antwerp. Later also to Hook of Holland and Rotterdam.		

12-12-1911 collision with HMS *Salmon*, 2 died on board *Salmon* and the others rescued by *Cambridge*. 25-11-1912 sold to Anglo Ottoman Steamship Co. (Ltd) (managers D. Lambiri), Greece and not renamed. 1919 sold to Administration de Navire a Vapeur Ottomane, Galata, Constantinople, Turkey and renamed *Gul Nehad*. 1922 sold to Adm. de Nav. a Vapeur Turque (Seiri Sefain), Galata, Constantinople, Turkey and renamed *Gulnihal*. 1937 sold for scrap.

117 COLCHESTER (master W. Nickerson) (sistership of *Cambridge*)

Gross tonnage	1160	Nett tonnage	517
Deadweight	907		
Dimensions	85,53m x 9,46m x 4,63m		
Engine	twin screw steamer further details see nr 116 Cambridge		
Capacity	730 passengers		
Builder	Earle's Co., Hull (312)		
Route	Harwich-Antwerp		

Maiden voyage 27-02-1889
1900 rebuilt engine room: 2 sets of T3 with 4cyl steam engines and was at that moment the only ship with T3 engines.
08-03-1916 in service Rotterdam-Tilbury (P.Q. was closed); 27-04-1916 with Captain Bennett, during the Rotterdam-Tilbury crossing, seized by the Germans and detained at Zeebrugge. The ship was captured there and the crew of 27 interned.
27-09-1916 torpedoed, when flying the German flag, by the Royal Navy. She was converted as mine-layer for the Baltic. After the war salvaged, towed back to England and scrapped.

118 CHELMSFORD (master J. Precious)

Gross tonnage	1635	Nett tonnage	596
Deadweight	1076		
Dimensions	91,60m x 10,50m x 4,93m		

Engine	Earle's Co., Hull, 2 xT3 4cyl 26", 39½", 61"-36"; 17½ knots; electric lights
Capacity	Particular and new was 2 beds per cabin, but the design was similar to *Ipswich*. On board there was a dining and a ladies saloon, smoke and stateroom and cabins for 200 passengers; each cabin with a ventilator connected to fresh air.
Launched	21-02-1893 by the Mayoress of Chelmsford
Builder	Earle's S & E Co., Hull (367)
Route	Harwich-Hook of Holland
Maiden voyage	31-0 5-18 93

06-1910 sold to Great Western Railway and renamed *Bretonne*, she served the Plymouth-Nantes freight route. This route ceased on 30-09-1911, after which the *Bretonne* was sold to Greece and renamed *Esperia*; 1920 renamed Syros.

1933 sold for scrap.

119 BERLIN (master J.Precious)

Gross tonnage	1745	Nett tonnage	556
Deadweight	1131		
Dimensions	92,21 m x 10,98m x 4,93m		
Engine	twin screw steamer built by Earle's Co., Hull, 2 x T3 4cyl 26", 39½", 6l"-36"; 18 knots		
Launched	1894		
Builder	Earle's Shipyard (379)		

10-01-1894 first arrival. She replaced *Princess of Wales*. Lloyds Register 1905; Gross tonnage 1775.

20-02-1907 sailed PQ22.00 with 91 passengers and 52 crew on board, under command of Captain J. Precious. The ship had rolled and pitched during the crossing. 21-02-1907 05.00 the passengers were already awake to prepare for disembarking. The Dutch pilot Brondes, Captain Precious and Chief Officer Morsley navigated the ship to the river entrance. When the *Berlin* passed the north mole, a heavy sea hit the port bow and swung her to the north. The northerly tide pushed the ship to the north and Captain Precious succeeded in turning the *Berlin*. She was then hit again by a heavy and high sea, which resulted in a grounding at the north mole. Several leaks sprung in ship's hull. Captain Precious' last effort to clear from this position was a double order on the telegraph 'full astern', without result. Shortly after the engines stopped and a 'black out' occurred. Chief Engineer Dennant came on the bridge and reported, that the boiler room was flooded and the fires extinguished. The ship's log: "06.35 *Berlin* grounded, heavy gale, tugs and lifeboats going out to assist. 08.25 position very dangerous, tried to get passengers off with tug and lifeboat, but have not succeeded". 09.30 *Berlin* broke in two, throwing passengers from the forward section into the icy water, only one of these was picked up alive, ss *Clacton*, en route for Rotterdam, arrived at the scene, she stood by for a time, but Captain Dale realised there was nothing they could do and so proceeded to Rotterdam. Ironically, serving on *ss Clacton* was AB-seaman Precious, son of Captain Precious. 10.26 the *Berlin* was declared total loss. Friday 22-02-1907 the gale ceased and the remaining survivors were rescued.

120 AMSTERDAM (master J. Chilver)

Gross tonnage	1745	Nett tonnage	556
Deadweight	1131		
Dimensions	92,21 m x 10,98m x 4,93m		
Engine	twin screw steamer details as nr 119 *Berlin*.		

	Consumption: 4 tons of coal/hour
Launched	24-01-1894
Builder	Earle's Shipyard, Hull (380).
First arrival	Harwich 28-04-1894
Maiden voyage	09-05-1894. She replaced the *Adelaide* nr 113
Crew	Captain + 2 nav. officers + 3 engineers + 3 petty officers + 1 steward + 20 AB Seamen +10 firemen + 8 greasers and 1 pilot.

23-01-1908, under command of Captain Richmond with 70 passengers and 50 crew on board, collided with ss *Axminster*. Passengers disembarked with boats and taken over by *Axminster*. *Amsterdam* steamed slowly to Hook of Holland and repairs at Rotterdam.

28-02-1913 first ship to use the new bunker machine at Parkeston.

10-1914 till 29-09-1919 requisitioned by the Royal Navy. 11-1919 again on the Hook-route.

12-1928 out of service and sold for scrap at Blyth.

121 VIENNA (master J.H.Robinson)

Gross tonnage	1753	Nett tonnage	550
Deadweight	1131		
Dimensions	92,21m x 10,98m x 4,93m		
Engine	twin screw steamer details as nr 119 *Berlin*		
Launched	18-07-1894		
Builder	Earle's Shipyard, Hull (387).		

11-10-1894 First arrival at Parkeston Quay. She replaced the *Claud Hamilton* nr 110.

Maiden voyage	25-10-1894

28/29-10-1908 took part in the search for ss *Yarmouth* but found only wreckage.

29-08-1914 till 12-12-1918 requisitioned by Royal Navy and renamed H.M.S. *Antwerp* and used against submarines.

1920 renamed by the G.E.R. *Roulers* and transferred to the Harwich-Zeebrugge service.

23-03-1930 sailed Parkeston Quay for the last time, heading for the breakers yard.

122 DRESDEN (master R.A. Henderson)

Gross tonnage	1805	Nett tonnage	496
Deadweight	1173		
Dimensions	92,14m x 11,62m x 4,96m		
Engine	twin screw steamer built by Earle's Co., Hull, 2 x T3 4cyl 26", & 63"-36"; abt 5000 hp; 18 knots. During trials 19 knots		
Launched	17-11-1896		
Builder	Earle's Shipyard, Hull (410), for the price of £63,750.		
Maiden voyage	29-06-1897 to Antwerp		

She was the last G.E.R. ship built by Earle's Co. at Hull. Originally equipped with Navy-funnel tops, later replaced by a new design, which became typical for the Great Eastern.

10-1913 disappearance of Dr. Rudolf Diesel, inventor of the diesel engine, from the ship during the night crossing from Hook of Holland to Harwich. 31-10-1914 requisitioned and renamed H.M.S. *Louvain* by the Royal Navy.

20-01-1918 sunk after an attack by German submarine UC 22 in the Eastern Mediterrnean.

123 CROMER (master W. Lucas)

Gross tonnage	812	Nett tonnage	253
Deadweight	706		
Dimensions	74,80m x 9,48m x 4,65m		
Engine	twin screw steamer built by Gourlay Bros. & Co., Dundee, 2 x T3 4cyl 15½", 25¼" & 41"-36"; 13½ knots; electric lights		
Launched	22-02-1902 by Miss A. Howard		
Builder	Gourlay's Yard , Dundee, (201); building costs £37,498.00 Maiden voyage 22-04-1902 to Rotterdam.		
Crew:	capt + 2 nav. officers + 2 engineers + 2 petty officers + 3 stewards + 8 AB Seamen + 9 firemen. Cargoholds for about 450 tons and 86 head of cattle		

She was the first freighter built for the G.E.R.
30-08-1934 sailed Parkeston Quay under tow of tug *Rozenburg* to Rotterdam breakers.

124 BRUSSELS (master J. Redwood)

Gross tonnage	1380	Nett tonnage	523
Deadweight	950		
Dimensions	87,00m x 10,37m x 4,73m		
Engine	twin screw steamer built by Gourlay Bros. & Co., Dundee, 2 x T3 4cyl 20", 33" & 54"-36"; 16 knots; electric lights		
Launched	25-03-1902 by Miss Drury		
Builder	Gourlay Bros. & Co., Dundee, (202), for the price of £63,700		
Maiden voyage	19-06-1902 to Antwerp		

First purpose built ship for the Antwerp service. This ship became famous through heroic actions of Captain Fryatt during the Great War. 28-03-1915 collided with the German submarine U 33 after an attack near Hook of Holland; 23-06-1916 captured by the Germans and seized at Zeebrugge-Captain Fryatt was arrested and later shot.

14-10-1917 scuttled in the entrance of Zeebrugge harbour during an attack by the Dover Patrol. 14-10-1919 the *Brussels* was raised. 08-1920 sold by G.E.R. for £3100 and finished her career as *Lady Brussels* on the west coast, between Liverpool and Dublin, as a cattle carrier
05-1929 sold for scrap to Port Glasgow.

125 YARMOUTH (master T. Stiff)

Gross tonnage	806	Nett tonnage	218
Deadweight	702		
Dimensions	74,80m x 9,48m x 4,65m		
Engine	twin screw steamer built by Gourlay Bros & Co., Dundee; 2 x T3 4cyl, 15½", 25¼" &41"-36"; 14 knots		
Launched	1903		
Builder	Gourlay Bros & Co., Dundee (208)		

Was last seen on the night of 27-10-1908 by the crew of Outer Gabbard Lightvessel, with a heavy list. Searched for by H.M.S. *Blake* and *Vienna*. One dead body was found, 21 crew and 1 passenger lost. Caxton Hall Inquiry provided that the ship went down due to heavy loads on deck. The insurance paid £5949.

126 CLACTON (master F. Lazell)

Gross tonnage	820	Nett tonnage	209
Deadweight	702		

Dimensions	74,73m x 9,48m x 4,63m		
Engine	twin screw steamer built by Earle's Co., Hull, 2 x T3 4cyl 15½", 25		

" & 4l"-36"; 14 knots

Launched	28-11-1904
Builder	Earle's Co., Hull (488)
Maiden voyage	07-02-1905

23-08-1906 grounded at the south mole at Hook of Holland during efforts to refloat the *Amsterdam*, which was grounded on the north mole, but refloated the same day.
07-10-1914 requisitioned and became a minesweeper. 22-10-1917 torpedoed in the Eastern Mediterranean by the German U 73, when attempting to protect H.M.S. *Grafton*.

127 NEWMARKET (master G. Fryatt)

Gross tonnage	833	Nett tonnage	192
Deadweight	721		
Dimensions	74,73m x 9,48m x 4,63m		
Engine	twin screw steamer built by Earle's Co., Hull, 2 x T3 4cyl 15½", 25¼" & 41"-36"; 14 knots		
Launched	11-07-1907		
Builder	Earle's Co., Hull (534)		
Entered service	08-1907		

08-10-1914 requisitioned as a minesweeper
16-07-1916 sunk in war service in the Dardanelles, Turkey.

128 COPENHAGEN (master L. Richmond)

Gross tonnage	2570	Nett tonnage	780
Deadweight	1498		
Dimensions	104,60m x 13,17m x 5,39m		
Engine	triple screw steamer built by John Brown & Co. Ltd, Clydebank, 3 Parsons turbines, direct drive, 5 boilers; 10,000 hp; 20 knots.		
Capacity	320 1st class cabin passengers, 130 2nd class cabin passengers		
Launched	22-10-1907 by Miss Ida Hamilton		
Builder	John Brown & Co. Ltd, Clydebank, (380)		

First arrival Parkeston on 24-01-1907

Maiden voyage	27-01-1907

Fitted out with wireless radio equipment. Interior made from mahogany and maplewood, dressed with crimson curtains. All cabins from passengers and crew fitted with telephone! 10-1914 in use as a hospital ship for the Admiralty. In 1916 in use as a hospital. 17-03-1917 sunk by torpedo in the North Sea, 5 lost.

129 MUNICH

Gross tonnage	2410	Nett tonnage	1019
Deadweight	1503		
Dimensions	104,60m x 13,17m x 5,39m		
Engine	triple screw steamer as detailed on *Copenhagen* nr 128		
Capacity	as nr 128.		
Launched	26-08-1908 by Miss Lawson, daughter of company director		
Builder	John Brown & Co. Ltd, Clydebank (384)		
Maiden voyage	16-11-1908		

12-10-1914 Requisitioned by the Admiralty and used as a hospital ship and trooper till the end of 1915. 1916 renamed *St. Denis* by the G.E.R. and joined the route Harwich-Hook of Holland again. After 1930 employed on Harwich-Zeebrugge service in the summer only.

10-05-1940 sailed Parkeston for Rotterdam to evacuate British subjects. 10-05-1940 scuttled by the crew in Rotterdam. Later raised by the Germans and used as a training vessel, renamed *Barbara*, later renamed *Schiff 52* and in use as auxiliary minesweeper.

1945 L.N.E.R. received her back in Kiel, Germany, and at the same time on hire to the local authorities as temporary shelter for homeless persons, later for students of the local university. 02-1950 towed back to England and scrapped at Sunderland.

130 ST. PETERSBURG (master W. Dale)

Gross tonnage	2448	Nett tonnage	1039
Deadweight	1502		
Dimensions	104,60m x 13,17m x 5,39m		
Engine	triple screw steamer as detailed for *Copenhagen* nr 128		
Launched	25-04-1910 by Miss Green		
Builder	John Brown & Co.Ltd, Clydebank (397)		

07-1910 arrived for the first time at Parkeston Quay

Maiden voyage	07-07-1910

04-08-1914 Britain and Germany declare war. On this day the German Ambassador in London with his staff of 120 persons travelled by a special train from London Liverpool Street Station to Harwich and embarked on board the *St. Petersburg* for the crossing to Hook of Holland. 12-10-1914 requisitioned for use as hospital ship. 18-10-1919 delivered back to G.E.R. and from November took up the Hook service again after rename to *Archangel*. After 1930 employed on Harwich-Zeebrugge service in the summer only. 10-12-1939 seized again and used as trooper between Southampton and Le Havre/Cherbourg

16-05-1941 bombed during the voyage from Kirkwall to Aberdeen with troops. Heavily damaged on tow and grounded; 17 lives lost.

131 STOCKHOLM

This ship, built as a sistership to *Copenhagen*, *Munich* and *St. Petersburg*, was sold at the yard. Twin screw steamer.

27-02-1917 the Admiralty seized the ship under construction. Launched 09-06-1917 as Stockholm; Builder John Brown & Co. Ltd., Clydebank, (431), originally for the Great Eastern Railway Co.

28-08-1917 renamed *Pegasus* and finished as an aircraft carrier.

08-1931 sold for scrap to Thos.W. Ward Ltd, Morecambe.

132 FELIXSTOWE

Gross tonnage	892	Nett tonnage	354
Deadweight	754		
Dimensions	65,60m x 10,12m x 7,09m		
Engine	single screw steamer built by Hawthorns & Co Ltd., Leith, T3cyl reciprocating machinery 21", 33" & 54"-36"; 12 knots		
Builder	1918 Hawthorns & Co. Ltd, Leith (147)		
Entered service	04-1919 on the Rotterdam service		

Bought for £70,049 on stocks and originally named *St. Nicholas*, but renamed *Felixstowe* by G.E.R.

1935 passed into the management of Associated Humber Lines and maintained the Harwich service.

03-08-1941 requisitioned by the Admiralty (Ministry of War Transport) and in 1942 renamed H.M.S. *Colchester*. In use for wreck removal at Harwich. 10-09-1946 delivered back to the L.N.E.R. and named again *Felixstowe*. 1948 moved to the

Weymouth-Channel Islands route (Western Region), later moved to Stranraer-Larne route. End 1950 sold to the Limerick Steamship Co. Ltd., Limerick, Ireland. 10-02-1951 sailed Parkeston Quay for the last time, heading for Emden (Germany) for dry docking and renaming to *Kylemore*.

22-11-1957 arrived for scrap at Hendrik Ido Ambacht, Holland, at the breakers yard of N.V. Holland.

133 KILKENNY/FRINTON

Gross tonnage	1361
Dimensions	82,22m x 11,03m x 4,96m
Engine	single screw steamer, T3cyl 26", 43" & 69"-42", 309 NHP, 15 knots
Launched	1903
Builder	Clyde Shipbuilding & Engineering Co. Ltd., Port Glasgow (254), originally for City of Dublin Steam Packet Co., Liverpool, (later known as B & I Lines) as Kilkenny.
Route	Liverpool-Dublin

1917 bought by G.E.R., but kept their own route.

15-05-1919 grounded in Knockadoon Bay, west of Youghal, during voyage from Liverpool to Cork in service of War Department. Repaired and 06-11-1919 renamed *Frinton* and entered service Harwich-Antwerp and Rotterdam, together with *Roulers*, *Marylebone* and *Woodcock*. 29-07-1929 sold to Greece to Inglessi Bros. and came in service between Piraeus and Brindisi, is not renamed. Later renamed *Samos* and owned by Samos Steam Nav. Co., service Venice and Ionian Islands. Later named *Frinton* again.

1941 lost by war action in Greek waters.

134 ST. GEORGE

Gross tonnage	2676
Dimensions	107,36m x 12,53m x 4,93m
Engine	triple screw steamer, 3 turbines (Parsons); 8 single ended boilers; 10,000 hp; 22½ knots
Builder	Cammell Laird & Co. Ltd., Birkenhead (665), originally for Fishguard & Rosslare Railways & Harbours Co., a subsidiary of the Great Western Railway Co.
Launched	13-01-1906

05-1913 sold to Canadian Pacific Railway and not renamed. Towed across the Atlantic Ocean for St. John-Digby service across the Bay of Fundy.

1915 returned to England and in use as hospital ship with 278 beds.

06-1919 sold to G.E.R. and refurbished. Accommodation for 500 passengers. 16-07-1929 last call at the Hook and sailed to Harwich. 16-10-1929 sailed Parkeston Quay for the breakers yard and scrapped by Hughes Bolckow Shipbreaking Co., Blyth.

135 ANTWERP

Gross tonnage	2957	Nett tonnage	1285
Deadweight	2373	Draft	4,07m
Dimensions	98,06m x 13,14m		
Engine	twin screw steamer built by John Brown & Co. Ltd., Clydebank, 4 turbines of 12.500 hp; 21 knots		
Launched	25-10-1919 by Lady Blythwood		
Builder	John Brown & Co. Ltd., Clydebank, (493). Sistership Bruges. Crew 60		

| Entered service | 06-1920 |
| Route | Harwich-Antwerp |

Originally built for the Antwerp route, but occasionally made trips on the Hook of Holland route.

28-06-1928 ship fitted with gramophones; 1939 as hotel ship at Parkeston Quay for Royal Navy personnel.

20-06-1940 arrived at St. Peter Port for the evacuation of the Channel Islands. 1941 rebuilt as escort ship and left Avonmouth for the Mediterranean. *Antwerp* was headquarters of Eastern Naval Task Force during the invasion of Sicily in 07-1943.

1945 redelivered to L.N.E.R., came into service as B.A.O.R.-ship on the Harwich-Hook of Holland.

19-09-1945 First trip ex Harwich; last trip ex Hook 01-05-1950. Laid up on the buoys of Parkeston Quay awaiting sale. 26-04-1951 sailed Parkeston Quay in tow to the breakers. Scrapped at Milford Haven by T.W. Ward Bros.

136 BRUGES

Gross tonnage	2949	Draft	4,07m
Dimensions	98,06m x 13,14m		
Engine	twin screw steamer, as detailed nr 135 Antwerp.		
Launched	20-03-1920		
Builder	John Brown & Co. Ltd, Clydebank (494)		
Route	Originally built for the Antwerp route, but made trips on the Hook of Holland route occasionally.		

27-09-1920 arrived Parkeston Quay 1st time. 05-07-1921 in service on the 'summer only' route Harwich-Zeebrugge. 28-06-1928 fitted with gramophones.

09-09-1939 requisitioned by the Royal Navy and used as trooper between Southampton and Le Havre/Cherbourg. Painted grey. 11-06-1940 bombed and sunk on the roads of Le Havre and 26-06-1940 declared total loss. Crew survived.

137 MALINES

Gross tonnage	2969	Nett tonnage	1262
Deadweight	2384	Draft	4,07m
Dimensions	97,78m x 13,14m		
Engine	twin screw steamer built by Wallsend Slipway & Engineering Co. Ltd., Newcastle, turbines Brown/Curtis geared, 12,500 hp; 21½ knots.		
Launched	06-01-1921		
Builder	High Walker Yard of Armstrong Whitworth & Co. Ltd., Newcastle (972)		
Sea trials	09-03-1921 – was the last ship delivered to the G.E.R.		
17-03-1921	1st arrival Parkeston Quay		
Entered service	21-03-1921		
Route	built for the Antwerp route, but made trips on the Hook of Holland route occasionally.		

Friday 08-07-1932 at anchor in the Schelde, next day collided at anchor with the German *Hanseat*. Heavily damaged, lifted anchor and grounded near Hoedekenskerke. Temporarily repaired and towed by six tugs to Antwerp for drydocking. 10-05-1940 sailed to Rotterdam for the evacuation of British civilians, including the crew of *St. Denis* (nr 129) and escaped from Hook of Holland. 22-07-1942 bombed by aircraft and grounded near Port Said (Egypt); 09-1943 salvaged, repaired and in service again; 1944 in use as training vessel in Kabret; end 1944 under management of General Steam Nav.Co.; 11-1945 arrived at the Tyne after a

voyage under tow of 6 months
24-04-1948 sold for scrap to Clayton & Davies Ltd. at Dunston.

138 SHERINGHAM

Gross tonnage	1088	Nett tonnage	429
Deadweight	950	Draft 4,47m	
Dimensions	78,08m x 11,01m		
Engine	single screw steamer built by Earle's Co. Ltd., Hull, T3cyl 22", 35" & 60"-39", coal fired; 14 knots		
Launched	1926		
Builder	Earle's Co. Ltd., Hull (669). The last ship built by this yard for L.N.E.R. Entered service 15-09-1926		
Route	Harwich-Rotterdam		

06-1940 in use during evacuation of the Channel Islands. Mostly in service during Second World War between Preston and Northern Ireland. 23-03-1946 first trip postwar Harwich-Rotterdam.

25-10-1958 arrived Parkeston Quay for the last time. 13-12-1958 sailed under tow to Belgium for scrap.

139 VIENNA

Gross tonnage	4227	Nett tonnage	1985
Deadweight	3028	Draft	4,65m
Dimensions	107,06m X 15,25m x 7,93		
Engine	twin screw steamer built by John Brown & Co. Ltd, Clydebank, turbines, Brown/ Curris geared, 5 boilers; 21 knots		
Capacity	444 1st class / 104 2nd class passengers		
Launched	10-04-1929		
Builder	John Brown & Co. Ltd, Clydebank (527)		
15-07-1929	Entered service		
Route	Harwich-Hook of Holland		

Designed by FW Noal and Capt. R Davies (Marine Superintendents). The first ferry with shop on board

1932 started cruising. In 1936, after of few years of experience with these cruises, the boat deck was extended to the aft-well to provide more sheltered space. This work was done at Parkeston Quay by the Marine Workshops. Last time at Hook of Holland prewar was 24-08-1939.

1940 requisitioned by Royal Navy. During the war in use as trooper. In service of the Ministry of War Transport from 1945 till 1960 as trooper between Harwich and Hook of Holland. First trip from Harwich to Hook of Holland on 01-08-1945. On 11-02-1952 boiler explosion, 2 killed; 02-07-1960 last arrival Parkeston Quay; 02-09-1960 sailed Parkeston Quay, under tow of tug *Merchantman* to Gent (Belgium)

04-09-1960 arrived Gent, scrapped by van Heyghen Freres.

140 PRAGUE

Gross tonnage	4220	Nett tonnage	1988
Deadweight	3028	Draft	4,27m
Dimensions	107,04m x 15,25m		
Engine	twin screw steamer as detailed for Vienna nr 139		
Launched	18-11-1929		
Builder	John Brown & Co. Ltd, Clydebank (528)		
Route	Harwich-Hook of Holland		

01-09-1939 last sailing from Hook of Holland prewar. 17-12-1939 seized by the Royal Navy; in use as trooper and hospital ship and completed 57 trips in dangerous circumstances. Wednesday 14-11-1945, 22.00 hours, sailed as first ship on the re-opened service to Hook of Holland (3 x per week); last sailing from Hook of Holland on 24-12-1947 (actually she was delayed and left 25-12-1947 about 02.15 hrs). Replaced by *Oranje Nassau*, she left the service for an overhaul at Clydebank. 14-03-1948 a fire broke out in the engine room, followed by an explosion. After that the ship listed to the quayside and sank. Declared total loss. 14-09-1948 arrived in Barrow for scrap.

141 AMSTERDAM

Gross tonnage	4218
Dimensions	107,04m x 15,25m x 4.27m
Engine	twin screw steamer as detailed for Vienna nr139
Capacity	246 1st class / 110 2nd class passengers Launched 13-01-1930
Builder	John Brown & Co. Ltd, Clydebank (529)
Maiden voyage	26-04-1930
31-08-1939	last trip sailed Hook of Holland

05-09-1939 requisitioned by the Royal Navy and in use as trooper. This ship was the last merchant ship that left Le Havre, before the enemy blew up the town; 06-1944 rebuilt as hospital ship; 07-08-1944 mined on the second trip as hospital ship near the French coast with heavy loss of life.

142 DEWSBURY

Gross tonnage	1686	Nett tonnage	907
Deadweight	1102	Draft	5,29m
Dimensions	80,83m x 10,99m		
Engine	single screw steamer built by Earle's Co.Ltd., Hull, T3cyl, 22", 35" & 60"-42"; 13 knots		
Capacity	32 crew, 456 passengers		
Launched	14-04-1910		
Builder	Earle's Co.Ltd., Hull (564), originally built for the Great Central Railway Co., service Grimsby-Hamburg.		
Entered service	17-06-1910		

11-11-1918 till 07-11-1919 used by G.E.R. as trooper Harwich-Rotterdam; 1923 G.C.R. amalgamated with L.N.E.R.; later rebuilt and reduced passenger capacity to 232; during Second World War in use between Fishguard and Rosslare, later in convoys across the Atlantic to Halifax and Gibraltar; 1946 in service on the Antwerp route. 10-02-1951 the Antwerp route terminated for passengers and the *Dewsbury* continued as a freighter with 12 passengers.
30-01-1959 last arrival at Parkeston Quay; 02-02-1959 left under tow to Flushing for scrap. Replaced by m.v. *Colchester* nr 148.

143 ACCRINGTON

Gross tonnage	1680	Nett tonnage	879
Deadweight	1098		
Dimensions	80,83m x 10,98m x 5,29m		
Engine	twin screw steamer built by Earle's Co. Ltd., Hull, T3cyl 22", 35" & 60"-42"; 2 boilers; 13 knots		
Launched	07-06-1910	Entered service	08-1910
Builder	Earle's Co. Ltd., Hull (565), originally for the Great Central Railway Co., Grimsby-Hamburg service		

11-11-1918 till 07-11-1919 used by G.E.R. as trooper Harwich-Rotterdam; 1923 owned by L.N.E.R.; this ship and the *Dewsbury* became famous for their luxury interiors with a 'stateroom' and a 'Ladies Lounge', finished with a writing table and a book case in mahogany etc.
1946 in service on the Antwerp route. 01-02-1951 passenger services to Antwerp ceased and the *Accrington* was laid-up for sale; 30-04-1951 sailed Parkeston Quay; 05-1951 arrived at Dunston for scrap.

144 ARNHEM

Gross tonnage	4891	Nett tonnage	2450
Dimensions	110,0m x 16,60m x 8,24m		
Engine	twin screw steamer built by John Brown & Co. Ltd., Clydebank; 2 sets Parsons direct geared turbines; 2 oilburned watertube boilers type Yarrow with 3 drums; 12480 hp; 21 knots		
Capacity	675 passengers including 576 in berths		
Launched	07-11-1946		
Builder	John Brown & Co. Ltd., Clydebank (636) as the last ship for the L.N.E.R.		
Maiden voyage	26-0 5-1947		

The ship was named after the town of Arnhem, where in Sept. 1944 the 1st Airborne Division resisted the German Army. During March, April and the first half of May 1954 she was converted to a 2-class vessel.

Lloyds Register	1963		
Gross tonnage	5008	Nett tonnage	2538
Deadweight	1139		

27-04-1968 last call at Hook of Holland and laid up; 13-08-1968 sailed Parkeston Quay; 16-08-1968 arrived Inverkeithing; sold to T.W. Ward Ltd. for scrap, which started 06-1969.

145 DUKE OF YORK

Gross tonnage	4325	Nett tonnage	1980
Draft	4,47m		
Dimensions	103,45m x 15,91m		
Engine	twin screw steamer built by Harland & Wolff Ltd, Belfast; 2 sets of turbines; 22 knots		
Launched	07-03-1935		
Entered service	06-1935		
Builder	Harland & Wolff Ltd., Belfast (951), originally built for London, Midland & Scottish Railway, port of registry: Lancaster		
Route	Heysham-Belfast		

During World War Two renamed HMS *Duke of Wellington* in Admiralty service. First trip from Harwich as trooper on 31-07-1945; last sailing from Hook of Holland as trooper on 14-11-1946;
10-1947 back in service in the Irish Sea; 31-05-1948 in use between Harwich and Hook of Holland and replaced *St. Andrew* and *Oranje Nassau*. In the summer of 1950 used by the Southern Region between Southampton and Cherbourg; during the winter 1950/1951 she had a major survey and a conversion at Harland & Wolff shipyards at Belfast, 2 funnels replaced by 1, boilers rebuilt from coal burning to oil burning, new extended capacity of 675 pass.; during the summer of 1951 used from Holyhead and later that year back in Harwich.
06-05-1953 collided with *Haiti Victory* during the crossing from Hook of Holland to Harwich. Ordered to abandon the ship, because she had lost the complete bow section. Towed to

Harwich. Repaired with a new bow section; re-entered service 25-01-1954 Harwich-Hook of Holland; 2,14m longer; 19-07-1963 last call at the Hook and sold to Chandris Line of Greece, renamed *York*. Sailed for Newcastle and rebuilt as cruise liner by Smith Dock.

15-03-1964 Maiden voyage from Venice as *Fantasia*.

1975 sold for scrap to Prodronos Sariktzis, Piraeus, Greece. 05-1976 scrapped.

146 AMSTERDAM

Gross tonnage	5092	Nett tonnage	2633
Deadweight	1113		
Dimensions	109,98m x 15,91m x 7,73m		
Engine	twin screw steamer built by John Brown & Co. Ltd., Clydebank, 2 sets of turbines and 2 water tube boilers; 21 knots		
Capacity	321 1st class and 236 2nd class berths, total 675		
Launched	19-01-1950		
Builder	John Brown & Co. Ltd, Clydebank (659)		
Entered service	29-05-1950 under command of Captain C. Baxter		
Route	Harwich-Hook of Holland		
Maiden voyage	10-06-1950 to the Hook		

07-11-1968 last voyage in day service, laid up; 01-05-1969 sailed P.Q. for Piraeus for transversion as a cruise liner; 13-05-1970 renamed *Fiorita* by owner Chandris Line.

09-05-1979 / 03-1983 laid up. 04-1983 sold to Ef-Em Handels GmbH, Munchen, Germany and directly resold to Sommerland Handels GmbH.

05-04-1983 arrived Kas (SW Turkey) and in use as hotelship 1987 sunk at the same place in Fethiye Port, SW Turkey. Small parts are still visible.

147 ISLE OF ELY

Gross tonnage	866	Nett tonnage	278
Deadweight	935	Draft	4,02m
Dimensions	73,76m x 11,44m		
Engine	motorship built by Ruston & Hornsby, Lincoln, 8cyl 4sa diesel; 13½ knots		
Builder	Goole Shipbuilding & Repair Co. Ltd., Goole (512)		
Entered service	27-10-1958 (Maiden voyage)		

Open shelter deck container ship; regularly used on the Rotterdam route; 1968 rebuilt as full containership, gross tonnage 1059; 1969 in service Holyhead-Dublin; 1972 Heysham-Belfast and Southampton-Channel Islands; 1973 Fishguard-Waterford; 1975 2 trips Harwich-Dunkirk; 11-1975 laid up for sale in Barrow; 1978 sold and renamed *Spice Island*; 1979 renamed *Spice Island Girl*;

29-03-1982 laid up at Portsmouth; 09-1984 sold for scrap to Brugge (Belgium).

148 COLCHESTER

Gross tonnage	866	Nett tonnage	278
Deadweight	935	Draft 4,02m	
Dimensions	73,76m x 11,44m		
Engine	motorship as detailed nr 147		
Builder	Goole Shipbuilding & Repair Co. Ltd., Goole (513)		
Entered service	21-01-1959		

Route regularly used on the Rotterdam route

Designed for general cargo, 1968 altered to a full container ship and after that in use between Weymouth and the Channel Islands. 1969 lengthened at Troon by 16.48m and returned to Harwich for the route to Zeebrugge. 1973 used in the Irish Sea between Holyhead and Dublin and Heysham-Belfast. 23-11-1973 chartered by Mc Andrew and used between Liverpool and Portugal and Spain. 03-1974 on charter to James Fisher, engine room fire suffered during bunkering. Repaired and laid up at Holyhead. 1975 sold to Cyprus and renamed *Taurus II*. 1979 renamed *Gloriana*. 1984 renamed *Sea Wave* and later renamed *Taurus*.

149 AVALON

Gross tonnage	6584	Nett tonnage	3542
Deadweight	842	Draft	4,82m
Dimensions	113,46m x 18,20m		
Engine	twin screw steamer built by A. Stephen & Sons Ltd., Glasgow, 2 sets of turbines and 2 watertube boilers; 15000 hp; 21 knots; 750 passengers.		
Launched	07-05-1963 without a christening ceremony		
Builder	Alexander Stephen & Sons Ltd., Glasgow (680)		

07-1963 arrived P.Q., christened there by Dr. Beeching, Chairman of British Railways, just after the centennial date of the route Harwich-Rotterdam to the first ship on this route. *Avalon* was at that moment the biggest vessel in the B.R. fleet, and the first full air-conditioned ship, equipped with stabilisers

04-1964 first cruise (weekend to Amsterdam); between 1964 and 1974 several cruises are made, eg. to North Cape, Leningrad and Casablanca. Christmas 1974 ended the service on the Hook route and left P.Q. to be rebuilt as ro/ro-vessel and survey at Swan Hunter Shipyard. As ro/ro vessel used between Fishguard-Rosslare and Holyhead-Dun Loaghaire.

1981 sold for scrap to Pakistan (Gadani Beach). For the last voyage renamed *Valon*, she sailed under her own power for the long journey to the breakers yard.

150 SEAFREIGHTLINER I

Gross tonnage	4043	Nett tonnage	2108
Deadweight	3295	Draft 4,42m	
Dimensions	111,56m x 16,79m		
Engine	twin screw motorship built by Mirrlees National Ltd, Stockport, 2 x 6cyl 4sa diesels; 4200 hp; full containership; 13½ knots		
Capacity	110 30' containers + 38 containers on deck		
Builder	J. Readhead & Sons Ltd., South Shields (621)		
Entered service	12-05-1968		
Routes	Harwich-Zeebrugge and Harwich-Rotterdam		
Maiden voyage	17-05-1968 to Zeebrugge		

30-07-1986 towed from P.Q. to River Blackwater and laid up; 09-02-1987 sailed to Falmouth (stores and bunkers); sailed to Naples (Italy); loaded there with electrical cables for China; 30-03-1987 sailed Colombo;

04-05-1987 arrived Kaohsiung (Taiwan) for scrap.

151 SEAFREIGHTLINER II

Gross tonnage	4034	Nett tonnage	2108
Deadweight	3265	Draft	4,42m
Dimensions	111,56m x 16,79m		

Engine	twin screw motorship as detailed nr 150
Launched	15-03-1968 by Mr. J.L. Harrington
Builder	J. Readhead & Sons Ltd., South Shields (622)
Entered service	03-06-1968
Routes	See nr 150

24-06-1968 Maiden voyage and inaugural journey Harwich-Rotterdam as full container line;

01-08-1986 towed from P.Q. to River Blackwater and laid up; 26-09-1986 sailed to Tilbury for a load of empty containers to Naples (Italy); 29-09-1986 sailed Tilbury; 08-10-1986 sailed Naples with a load of pipelines for scrap; 02-01-1987 arrived Karachi (Pakistan) and beached on arrival. Demolition started before the crew had left the ship.

152 ST. GEORGE

Gross tonnage	7356	Nett tonnage	3869
Deadweight	1036	Draft	5,03m
Dimensions	115,22m x 20,60m		
Engine	twin screw motorship built by Ruston & Hornsby, 4 x 9cyl 2sa diesels, 18000 hp; 21 knots		
Capacity	1200 passengers-560 berths/640 deck		
Launched	28-02-1968 by Mrs. H. Johnson, wife of the new Chairman of B.R.		
Builder	Swan Hunter & Tyneside Shipbuilders, Tyneside (2029)		
Entered service	13-07-1968;		
Route	Harwich-Hook of Holland		
Maiden voyage	17-07-1968 to Hook of Holland		

Ship was the first ro/ro passenger ferry of the B.R. fleet in Harwich; This ship made 3995 trips (7628 crossings) to the Netherlands, before she ceased service, plus 5 trips to Amsterdam 05-06-1983 last sailing from Hook of Holland.

After being laid up in the River Fal since November 1983 she was sold to Ventouris Line of Greece on 18 September 1984 and renamed *Patra Express* for service between Patra and Bari. In 1988 was re-engined with Wartsila diesels. In February 1990 she was subject to an abortive sale to British Iberian Lines who planned to rename the ship *Maiden Castle* for service between Poole - Bilbao. She was sold to SeaEscape in March 1990 and rebuilt as a cruise ship at Humber Ship Repair, Immingham between April and July. Renamed *Scandinavian Sky II* and then *Scandinavian Dawn* she was operating as a one-day casino cruise ship between Fort Lauderdale - Freeport from August 1990. From the mid 1990's she cruised from ports within Florida and the Gulf of Mexico on a variety of routes and names. In November 1996 she was renamed *Discovery Dawn* and in May 1998 was known as Island Dawn. August 1999 saw her as *Discovery Dawn* whilst from July 2000 onwards she became the *Texas Treasure*. Her latter years in service were as a casino ship based at Corpus Christi and then Port Aransas in Texas. In May 2008 she suffered from machinery faults deemed uneconomic to repair and so in July 2008 she was sold for breaking up in India.

153 ST. EDMUND

Gross tonnage	8987	Nett tonnage	4697
Deadweight	1830	Draft	5,20m
Dimensions	119,51m x 22,64m		
Engine	twin screw motorship built by Stork Werkspoor, Amsterdam, 4 x 8cyl 4sa diesels, type TM 410; 20400 hp; 21 knots		
Capacity	1400 passengers-671 berths/729 deck		

Launched	14-11-1973 by Mrs Caroline Marsh, wife of B.R. Chairman
Builder	Cammell Laird Shipbuilders Ltd., Birkenhead(1361)
Owned by	Passtruck (Shipping) Co. Ltd., London (subsidiary of B.R.)

24-12-1974 First arrival Parkeston Quay

Route	Harwich-Hook of Holland
Maiden voyage	19-01-1975 to Hook of Holland

12-05-1982 requisitioned by the Admiralty for use as a troop ship between United Kingdom/Ascension and the Falkland Islands, during the crisis with Argentina; 20-05-1982 sailed from Devonport to Ascension, under command of Captain M. Stockman and Chief Engineer J. Fletton; the *St. Edmund* transported General Menendez with 1500 troops back to Argentina; in Port Stanley Prince Andrew used the SATCOM telephone for contact with Buckingham Palace, just after the birth of Prince William. The ship was a ferry between Port Stanley and Ascension Island and as a hotel ship at Port Stanley; she gained the nickname: 'The Stanley Hilton', because of the good meals, accommodation and hospitality.

28-02-1983 back in England for a survey at Wallsend. Sold by Sealink (UK) Ltd to Ministry of Defence, renamed HMS *Keren* and retained on the Falkland-Ascension supply link under the management of Blue Star.

1985 sold to Cenargo Navigation Ltd., renamed *Scirocco* and returned to ferry work in the Mediterranean in the summer of 1986. She served several services there until the end of 1988.

21-02-1989 entered service between Poole and the Channel Islands for British Channel Island Ferries as a long term charter from Cenargo Navigation Ltd. and renamed *Rozel*, registration Bahamas. This charter lasted until 18 January 1992. Next day she was renamed back to *Scirocco* and later chartered to Trasmediterranea of Spain for service between Malaga and Melilla. The next ten years were years of extensive chartering. In 1993 she sailed for FerriMaroc out of Spain between Almeria and Nador, then again for Compagnie Marocaine de Navigation of Morocco to sail Nador to Port Vendres. The following year saw her back with Cotunav of Tunisia sailing between Tunis and Genoa until November 1994 when she returned to Ferrimaroc to sail for the next 9 years on the Nador to Almeria route. In April 2004 she was sold to El Salam Maritim of Cairo in Egypt who then registered her in Panama and renamed her *Santa Catherine 1*. In June 2004 she was chartered to sail between Nador and Almeria for Compagnie Marocaine de Navigation of Morocco whilst in 2005 she sailed for Algerie Ferries. Towards the end of 2005 she sailed from Suez as a pilgrim ship and then on 30 May 2006 she was renamed as *Sara 3*. She came out of service during 2008 and in June 2009 she was sold to be broken up in India.

154 ST. NICHOLAS

Gross tonnage	17043	Nett tonnage	7859
Draft	6,10m		
Dimensions	149m x 26m		
Engine	twin screw motorship, Wartsila, 4 x diesels; 15360 hp; 20, 4 knots		
Capacity	2100 passengers-1061 berths; 480 cars		
Originally named: *Prinsessan Birgitta*			
Builder	Arendalsvarvet Shipyard in Gothenburg (Sweden) (909) and taken over by Stena Line during construction; originally ordered by		

	Sessan Line in 01-1979; completed 12-1981
Maiden voyage	03-06-1982 between Gothenburg and Frederikshavn

Until 28-02-1983; chartered by Sealink (UK) Ltd after refitting at the Cityvarvet Shipyard in Gothenburg, she was renamed *St. Nicholas*;

10-06-1983 maiden voyage to Hook of Holland; 1987 property of Finance Ltd, Squarehorn Ltd, Elstree Platform Ltd and A. Moir & Co Ltd in the United Kingdom. 1988 Bahamas registration; 1989 owned by a subsidiary of Rederi AB Gotland in Visby; 01-1991 renamed *Stena Normandy*;

19-06-1991 last call in Hook of Holland and replaced by the *Stena Britannica*; transferred to Southampton and started a new route to Cherbourg.

19 June 1991 - Last day of service between Harwich - Hook of Holland.

28 June 1991 in service between Southampton - Cherbourg until 29 November 1996.

January 1997 saw her chartered to Hansatee Oy, Tallinn, renamed Normandy and from 23 April 1997 in service between Tallinn - Helsinki. January 1998 was chartered to Irish Ferries, Dublin for the route between Rosslare - Pembroke Dock. 10 November 1999 sold to Irish Continental Ferries, Dublin. January 2000 refitted in Poland and re-entered service in March mainly from Rosslare to Cherbourg until 4 November 2007. Laid up in Fredericia and sold 28 January 2008 to Equinox Offshore Accommodation Ltd, Singapore. After a summer season charter to Ferrimaroc between Almeria and Nador she arrived 19 October 2008 in Singapore for conversion to an offshore Accommodation and Repair Vessel (as ARV2). Conversion still awaiting. Scrapped, after arriving at Alang on 30th November 2012.

BAREBOAT-CHARTERED VESSELS OF SEALINK STENA LINE LTD/ STENA SEALINK LTD, HARWICH.

(Time-chartered by Stena Line BV, Hook of Holland)

51 STENA NORMANDY

(see nr 154)

52 STENA BRITANNICA

Gross tonnage	26671	Nett tonnage
14378		
Draft	6,70m	
Dimensions	166,1m x 28,40m	
Engine	twin screw motorship, Wartsila Pielsrick, 4 x type 12 PC 2.5V diesels; 31200 hp; 22 knots	
Capacity	1800 passengers; 647 cabins with 1600 berths; 450 cars	
Owner	Stena Rederi AB, Gothenburg. Swedish registration.	
Builder	Oy Wartsila AB in Turku Abo (Finland) (1252)	

Originally built 1981 for Silja Line as operator as *Silvia Regina*, together with her sistership *Finlandia*, for the run across the Baltic between Stockholm and Helsinki; owned by Finland Steamship Company (EFFOA)/Johnson Line of Stockholm. 1988 bought by Stena Rederi AB and chartered back to Silja Line. 1991 replaced by *Silja Symphony*; 05-1991 refitted at Bremerhaven for use on the Harwich-Hook of Holland route and renamed *Stena*

Britannica. 19-06-1991 the 1st call at Hook of Holland, after berthing trials in Hook of Holland on 17-06-1991. 19 June 1991 in service between Hook of Holland - Harwich. 3 March 1994 was her last day on the route. She left Hoek for Frederikshavn, was transferred to Stena Rederi AB and renamed *Stena Saga*. 5 March 1994 she started on the route between Frederikshavn and Oslo. She was rebuilt in February 2000 at the City yard, Gothenburg to fit new sponsons and following various other refits she is still in service on the same route.

TRAIN FERRIES ON THE HOOK OF HOLLAND-HARWICH SERVICE

From time to time extra freight ships were required to operate on the Harwich-Hook service and rather than charter specialist vessels, it was the practice of British Rail, and later Sealink UK Ltd., to transfer one of their train ferry vessels from the Harwich-Zeebrugge route. The first such vessel to call at the Hook was the *Essex Ferry* on 9th November 1968 in order to pick up a large number of redundant wooden railway containers. They were surplus to requirements due to the commencement of the new Harwich-Rotterdam container service which used standard ISO containers.

The *Essex Ferry* did not fit the Hook of Holland linkspan and so the old containers were crane loaded.

In the seventies and eighties the 'Essex' and the other three Harwich train ferries were occasionally switched to serve the Hook in their capacities as cargo ships and transporters of trade cars and heavy ro-ro freight. The *Cambridge Ferry* was the final vessel of this class to call at the Hook on 7th March 1986 when carrying freight during the absence of the *St. Nicholas* which was on annual overhaul.

One more vessel brought in to carry extra freight was the chartered Stena Line ro-ro ship *Stena Sailer* which appeared again during 1986. She later became Sealink's *St. Cybi* and was based on the Welsh port of Holyhead.

PRINCIPAL VESSELS USED BY STENA LINE BV ON THE HARWICH-HOOK ROUTE SINCE 1994.

ST. NICHOLAS / STENA NORMANDY (IMO: 7901772)

Built: 1981 by Götaverken Arendal Ab Gothenburg, Sweden - yard no. 909.

Dimensions: 149.03 x 26.01 x 6.10 m.   Tonnage: 14368 gt.

Engines: Four Nohab-Wärtsilä Vasa 12V32A diesels.

Power Output: 15360 kW.   Speed: 20.0 knots.

Passengers: 2100

(1983 - rebuilt as a night ferry at Götaverken City Shipyard, Gothenburg. Tonnage revised to 17043 gt).

Cabin berths: 400. After 1983: 1061.

Freight capacity: 1260 lane metres or 700 cars or 70 x 15m lorries. After 1983: 900 lane metres or 460 cars or 52 x 15m lorries and 16 cars.

Date of first sailing as *St. Nicholas* (with Sealink): 9th June 1983

Date of first sailing re-named as *Stena Normandy*: 21st January 1991

Date of last sailing in service: 19th June 1991

Transferred to Stena Line UK, Southampton - Cherbourg

Former names: *Prinsessan Birgitta* (1981), *St. Nicholas* (1983)

Top: The **Stena Scotia** and **Stena Transit** at the Hook of Holland. (Rob de Visser)

Above: The **Somserset** arriving in the New Waterway. (Rob de Visser)

Right: The much travelled **Stena Nordica** covered the Harwich-Hook service in 2020. (Rob de Visser)

Names since leaving Stena Line BV: *Stena Normandy* (1991), *Normandy* (1997), (since March 2008 IMO:8000923)

Sister ship: *Kronprinsessan Victoria*

KONINGIN BEATRIX (IMO: 8416308)

Built: 1986 by Van der Giessen de Noord, Krimpen a/d Ijssel, Holland - yard no. 935.

Dimensions: 161.78 x 24.60 x 6.20 m.   Tonnage: 31189 gt.

Engines: Four 8L40/45 MAN diesels.

Power Output: 19360 kW.   Speed: 20.0 knots.

Passengers: 2100.   Cabin berths: 1188.

Freight capacity: 900 lane metres or 500 cars or 80 lorries and 225 cars.

Date of first sailing with SMZ: 22nd April 1986

Date of last sailing in service: 1st June 1997

Transferred to Stena Line UK, Fishguard-Rosslare

Names since leaving Stena Line BV: *Stena Baltica* (2002). Names since leaving Stena Line *Snav Adriatic (*2013). Still in service: With GNV - Naples to Palermo

---

STENA SEATRADER (IMO: 7301491)

Built: 1973 by A/S Nakskov Skibsværft, Nakskov, Denmark - yard no. 199.

Dimensions: 148.01 x 22.13 x 5.54 m. (1982 - Lengthened, rebuilt and re-engined at Howaldtswerke / Deutsche Werft AG, Hamburg, Germany. After lengthening: 182.73 x 22.13 x 6.22m).

Tonnage: 5159 gt. (After 1982: 6962 gt).

Engines: Four Lindholmen Semt-Pielstick 6PC2L/8 diesels. (After 1982: Two Pielstick 26L diesels).

Power Output: 14000 hp (After 1982: 10298 kW).

Speed: 18.5 knots (After 1982: 17.5 knots).

Passengers: 36 (After 1982: 236).

Cabin Berths: 36 (After 1982: 236).

Freight capacity: 18 lorries plus 578 metres of rail track.

Further rebuilt in 1987 at Oy Wärtsilä Ab, Turku, Finland. (Tonnage: re-rated at 17991 gt). Freight capacity: 2100 lane metres or 170 x 12m trailers.

Date of first sailing in Stena Line BV service: 2nd May 1990

Date of last sailing in service: 11th August 2006

Transferred to Stena Line UK, Holyhead - Dublin

Former names: *Svealand* (1973), *Svealand of Malmo* (1982), *Svea Link* (1987), *Stena Seatrader* (1990)

Names since leaving Stena Line BV: *Seatrade* (2008). Scrapped, after arriving at Alang on 14th January 2012.

Sister ships: *Gotaland*

STENA BRITANNICA (IMO: 7911545)

Built: 1981 the hull by Oy Wärtsilä Ab, Perno, Finland. Equipped at Oy Wärtsilä Ab City Shipyard, Turku, Finland - yard no 1252.

Dimensions: 166.10 x 28.46 x 6.70 m.   Tonnage: 25905 gt.

Engines: Four Wärtsilä-Pielstick 12PC2-5V diesels.

Power Output: 22948 kW.   Speed: 22.0 knots.

Passengers: 2000.   Cabin berths: 1601.

Freight capacity: 450 cars or 70 trucks.

Date of first sailing in Stena Line BV service: 19th June 1991

Date of last sailing in service: 3rd March 1994

Transferred to Stena Line AB, Oslo-Frederikshavn. Since March 1994: In service with Stena Line - Oslo to Fredrikshavn but currently laid up.

Former names: *Silvia Regina*

Names since leaving Stena Line BV: *Stena Saga*,

Sister ship: *Finlandia*

STENA EUROPE (IMO: 7901760)

Built: 1981 by Götaverken Arendal Ab Gothenburg, Sweden - yard no. 908.

Dimensions: 149.05 x 26.55 x 6.12 m.   Tonnage: 14378 gt.

Engines: Four Nohab-Wärtsilä Vasa 12V32A diesels.

Power Output: 15360 kW.   Speed: 20.5 knots.

Passengers: 2100 (1982 - rebuilt as a night ferry at Götaverken City Shipyard, Gothenburg. Tonnage revised to 17062 gt).

Cabin berths: 400. After 1983: 1332.

Freight capacity: 1260 lane metres or 700 cars or 70 x 15m lorries. After 1982: 900 lane metres or 420 cars or 68 x 12m trailers.

Date of first sailing in Stena Line BV service: 4th March 1994

Date of last sailing in service: 1st June 1997

Transferred to Lion Ferries, Karlskrona - Gdynia. Still in service: With Stena Line - Fishguard to Rosslare.

Former names: *Kronprinsessan Victoria* (1981), *Stena Saga* (1988).

Names since leaving Stena Line BV: *Lion Europe* (1997), *Stena Europe* (1998).

Sister ship: *Prinsessan Birgitta*

ROSEBAY (IMO: 7429229)

Built: 1976 by JJ Siete Werft, Hamburg, Germany - yard no. 792.

Dimensions: 135.49 x 21.71 x 6.46 m.   Tonnage: 5631 gt.

Engines: Two MAN 6-52/55A diesels.

Power Output: 9312 kW.   Speed: 19.0 knots.

Passengers: 63.   Cabin Berths: 63.

Freight capacity: 1624 lane metres or 135 x 12m trailers.

(Passenger capacity later revised to 150 with 107 cabin berths, Tonnage 13700 gt)

Date of first sailing in Stena Line BV service: 4th July 1994

(Left 1st May 1997, returned 8th June 1998)

Date of last sailing in service: 13th March 2001

Went off charter, sold to Rederi Ab Engship for service in the Baltic. Scrapped, after arriving at Alang on 24th May 2014.

Former names: *Transgermania* (1976), *Rosebay* (1993), *Eurostar* (1995), *Eurocruiser* (1997), *Rosebay* (1998).

Names since leaving Stena Line BV: *Transparadan* (2001), *Translandia* (2004).

STENA SEARIDER (IMO: 6915881)

Built: 1969 by Oy Wärtsilä Ab, Helsinki, Finland - yard no. 390.

Dimensions: 137.34 x 24.54 x 5.20 m. (1986 - Lengthened and rebuilt at Wärtsilä Marine Inc. Turku, Finland. After lengthening: 178.69 x 24.60 x 5.50 m).

Tonnage: 6209 gt. (After 1986: 20914 gt).

Engines: Two Wärtsilä-Pielstick 12 PC2V-400 diesels.

Power Output: 9936 kW).   Speed: 18.0 Knots.

Passengers: 36   Cabin Berths: 36

(After 1986: 150)   (After 1986: 150)

(Passenger capacity revised to 120 with 105 cabin berths)

Date of first sailing in Stena Line BV service: 2nd May 1997

Freight capacity: 2390 lane metres or 198 x 12m trailers.

Date of last sailing in service: 18th June 2007

Laid up in Rotterdam and later sold to Ustica Lines, Italy. Scrapped, after arriving at Aliaga on 11th July 2014.

Former names: *Finncarrier* (1969), *Polaris* (1976), *Scandinavia* (1984), *Scandinavian Link* (1986), *Stena Searider* (1990), *Searider* (1991), *Stena Searider* (1992), *Norse Mersey* (1992), *Stena Searider* (1995)

Names since leaving Stena Line BV: *Claudia M* (2007)

HSS STENA DISCOVERY (IMO: 9107590)

Built: 1997 by Finn Yards, Rauma, Finland - yard no. 406.

Dimensions: 126.60 x 40.00 x 4.80 m.   Tonnage: 19638 gt.

Engines: Two General Electric LM 2500 and Two General Electric LM 1600 gas turbines.

Power Output: 78000 kW.   Speed: 40.0 knots.

Passengers: 1500.

Freight capacity: 885 lane metres for either 375 cars or 50 trucks and 100 cars.

Date of first sailing in Stena Line BV service: 2nd June 1997

Date of last sailing in service: 8th January 2007

Laid up in Belfast and later sold to Albamar SA in Venezuela. Scrapped, after arriving at Aliaga on 26th July 2015.

Names since leaving Stena Line BV: *HSS Discovery* (2009)

Sister ships: *Stena Explorer* and *Stena Voyager*

STENA BRITANNICA (IMO: 9145164)

Built: 2000 by Astilleros Españoles, Puerta Real, Spain - yard no. 80.

Dimensions: 188.30 x 28.70 x 6.15 m.   Tonnage: 30500 gt.

Engines: Four Sulzer 8ZAL40S diesels.

Power Output: 23040 kW.   Speed: 22.0 knots.

Passengers: 452.   Cabins: 192.

Cabin Berths: 452.

Freight capacity: 2500 lane metres or 160 x 15m lorries.

Date of first sailing in Stena Line BV service: 3rd October 2000

Date of last sailing in service: 25th February 2003

Sold to Finnlines for service between Germany and Finland. Still in service: With Finnlines - Naantali to Kapellskar

Names since leaving Stena Line BV: *Finnfellow*

Sister ships: *Finnclipper, Finneagle, Stena Hollandica*

STENA HOLLANDICA (IMO: 9145176)

Built: 2001 by Astilleros Españoles, Puerta Real, Spain - yard no.81.

Dimensions: 188.30 x 28.70 x 6.15 m. (2007 - Lengthened at Lloyd Werft, Bremerhaven, Germany. After lengthening : 240.10 x 28.70 x 6.15 m).

Tonnage: 30500 gt. (After 2007: 44372 gt).

Engines: Four Sulzer 8ZAL40S diesels.

Power Output: 23040 kW.   Speed: 22.0 knots.

Passengers: 452   Cabins: 192
(After 2007: 900)   (After 2007: 398)

Cabin Berths: 452 (After 2007: 994).

Freight capacity: 2500 lane metres or 160 x 15m lorries. (After 2007: 3980 lane metres or 260 x 15m lorries).

Date of first sailing in Stena Line BV service: 9th March 2001

Date of last sailing in service: 15th May 2010

Transferred to Stena Line AB, Kiel - Gothenburg. Still in service: With Stena Line - Gothenburg to Kiel

Names since leaving Stena Line BV: *Stena Germanica* (2010)

Sister ships: *Finnclipper, Finneagle, Finnfellow*

STENA BRITANNICA (IMO: 9235517)

Built: 2003 by Hyundai Heavy Industries, South Korea - yard no. 1392.

Dimensions: 211.56 x 29.30 x 6.30 m. (2007 - Lengthened at Lloyd Werft, Bremerhaven, Germany. After lengthening: 240.10 x 29.30 x 6.30 m).

Tonnage: 43490 gt. (After 2007: 55050 gt).

Engines: Four MAN B&W 9L40/54 diesels.

Power Output: 25920 kW.   Speed: 22.5 knots.

Passengers: 900   Cabins: 246
(After 2007: 900)   (After 2007: 395)

Cabin Berths: 600 (After 2007: 986).

Freight capacity: 3400 lane metres or 200 x 15m lorries. (After 2007: 4100 lane metres or 230 x 15m lorries plus 170 cars)

Date of first sailing in Stena Line BV service: 25th February 2003

Date of last sailing in service: 8th October 2010

Transferred to Stena Line AB, Kiel - Gothenburg. Still in service: With Stena Line - Gothenburg to Kiel

Names since leaving Stena Line BV: *Stena Scandinavica* (2010)

Sister ships: *Stena Adventurer*

NEW SUPERFERRIES

STENA HOLLANDICA (IMO: 9419163)

Built: 2010 Wadan Yards, Wismar, Germany - yard no.159.

Dimensions: 240.00 x 32.00 x 6.40 m.   Tonnage: 63039 gt.

Engines: Two MAN 8L48/60 and Two MAN 6L48/60 diesels.

Power Output: 33600 kW.   Speed: 22.0 knots.

Passengers: 1200.   Cabins: 538.

Cabin Berths: 1253.

Freight capacity: 5500 lane metres or 300 x 15m lorries plus 230 cars.

Date of first sailing in Stena Line BV service: 16th May 2010

Sister ship: *Stena Britannica*

STENA BRITANNICA (IMO: 9419175)

Built: 2010 Wadan Yards, Wismar, Germany - yard no.164.

Dimensions: 240.00 x 32.00 x 6.40 m.   Tonnage: 63039 gt.

Engines: Two MAN 8L48/60 and Two MAN 6L48/60 diesels.

Power Output: 33600 kW.   Speed: 22.0 knots.

Passengers: 1200.   Cabins: 538.

Cabin Berths: 1253.

Freight capacity: 5500 lane metres or 300 x 15m lorries plus 230 cars.

Date of first sailing in Stena Line BV service: 9th October 2010

Sister ship: *Stena Hollandica*

PRINCIPAL VESSELS USED BY STENA LINE BV ON THE HARWICH-ROTTERDAM ROUTE.

STENA TRANSFER (IMO: 7528570)

Built: 1977 by Hyundai Shipbuilders & Heavy Industries, Ulsan, South Korea - yard no. 643.

Dimensions: 151.94 x 21.67 x 6.50 m. (1979: Rebuilt and lengthened at Hapag Lloyd Werft GmbH, Bremerhaven, Germany. After lengthening 184.61 x 25.28 x 6.37 m).

Tonnage: 5724 gt. (After 1979: 6455 gt).

Engines: Two Pielstick 12PC2-5V diesels.

Power Output: 11475 kW. | Speed: 17.0 knots.

Passengers: 12. (After 1979: 144) | Cabin Berths: 12. (After 1979: 144)

Freight capacity: 1450 lane metres. (After 1979: 2382 lane metres.

Former names: *Stena Runner* (1977), *Alpha Progress* (1978), *Hellas* (1979), *Doric Ferry* (1986), *European Tideway* (1992), *Ideway* (2002), *Stena Transfer* (2002)

STENA PARTNER (IMO: 7528635)

Built: 1978 by Hyundai Shipbuilders & Heavy Industries, Ulsan, South Korea - yard no. 649.

Dimensions: 151.94 x 21.67 x 6.50 m. (1979 - Rebuilt at LloydWerft GmbH, Bremerhaven, Germany. After rebuild: 151.94 x 25.28 x 6.52 m).

Tonnage: 5456 gt. (After 1979: 6455 gt).

Engines: Two Pielstick 12PC2-5V diesels.

Power Output: 11475 kW. | Speed: 17.0 knots.

Passengers: 12. (After 1979: 210) | Cabin Berths: 12. (After 1979: 210)

1981: Lengthened at Hapag Lloyd Werft GmbH, Bremerhaven. (After lengthening: 184.61 x 25.28 x 7.27 m., Tonnage: 8596 gt.)

Former names: *Alpha Enterprise* (1978), *Syria* (1979), *Stena Transporter* (1983), *Cerdic Ferry* (1985), *European Freeway* (1992), *Freeway* (2002), *Stena Partner* (2003)

Last day in service: 20th December 2010 Names since leaving Stena Line BV: *Sea Partner* (2010). Still in service: With SeaLine - Constanta - Karasu - Chornomorsk (Black Sea).

STENA TRANSPORTER (IMO: 7528659)

Built: 1978 by Hyundai Shipbuilders & Heavy Industries, Ulsan, South Korea - yard no. 651.

Dimensions: 151.94 x 21.67 x 6.45 m. (1981: Rebuilt at Hapag Lloyd Werft GmbH, Bremerhaven, Germany. After rebuild: 151.94 x 25.28 x 6.52 m).

Tonnage: 5539 gt. (After 1981: 6455 gt).

Engines: Two Pielstick 12PC2-5V diesels.

Power Output: 11475 kW. | Speed: 17.0 knots.

Passengers: 12. (After 1981: 144) | Cabin Berths: 12. (After 1981: 144)

Freight capacity: 1450 lane metres. (After 1981: 1650 lane metres).

1986: Rebuilt at Wilton Feyenoord Rotterdam BV, Holland as a passenger ferry. (Revised tonnage: 18732 gt., Passengers: 688., Cabin berths: 258).

1995: Rebuilt at Harland & Wolf, Belfast and converted back to a freight ferry. (Revised tonnage: 16776 gt., Passengers: 220., Cabin berths: 220).

Former names: *Merzario Espania* (1978), *Merzario Hispania* (1978), *Nordic Ferry* (1980), *Pride of Flanders* (1992), *Flanders* (2002), *Stena Transporter* (2002)

Last day in service: 1st March 2009. Sold to Stradablu of Italy and renamed *Strada Corsa* (2009). Other names: *La Paz Star* (2013), *Med Star* (2016), *Star* (2017). Scrapped, after arriving at Aliaga on 6th December 2017

Sister ships common to all three - (in order of first built)

Merzario Ausonia, Elk, Stena Prosper, Stena Project, Tor Felicia, Norsky, Imparca Express 1 and *Stena Trader*

Date of first sailing in Stena Line BV service: All three ships were officially taken over from P&O European Ferries on 31st July 2002 and retained in service on the route between Felixstowe and Rotterdam. This was later transferred to a Harwich - Rotterdam service on 15th September 2002.

Both *Stena Transfer* and *Stena Partner* had by then a re-rated tonnage of 21162 gt, a freight capacity of 2450 lane metres or 180 x 12m trailers and passenger accommodation for 166 persons.

The *Stena Transporter* had been re-rated at 16776 gt, with a freight capacity of 1850 lane metres or 122 x 12m trailers and accommodation for 124 passengers.

Last day in service: *Stena Transporter* 1st March 2009.
Sold to Stradablu of Italy and renamed *Strada Corsa* (2009)
Last day in service: *Stena Transfer:* 6th September 2010
Sold for scrapping in China
Last day in service: *Stena Partner:* December 2010

STENA CARRIER (IMO: 9138800)

Built: 1998 the hull by Societa Esercizio Cantieri S.p.A, Viareggio, Italy - yard no.1548. Equipped in 2003 at Nuovi Cantieri Apuania, Spa, La Spezia, Italy.

Dimensions: 183.00 x 25.50 x 7.40 m.

Tonnage: 21104 gt.

Engines: Four Sulzer 8ZA40S diesels.

Power Output: 23040 kW. | Speed: 21.0 knots.

Passengers: 12. | Cabin Berths: 12.

Freight capacity: 2715 lane metres or 225 x 12m trailers.

Date of first sailing in Stena Line BV service: 6th September 2010

Former names: *Aronte* (1998), *Stena Carrier II* (2004).

Sister shipsß: *Stena Freighter, Ark Forwarder*

STENA FREIGHTER (IMO: 9138795)

Built: 1998 the hull by Societa Esercizio Cantieri S.p.A, Viareggio, Italy - yard no. 1547. Equipped in 2003 at Elektromehanika D.o.o. Rijeka, Croatia.

Dimensions: 182.00 x 26.00 x 7.40 m. | Tonnage: 21104 gt.

Engines: Four Sulzer 8ZA40S diesels.

Power Output: 23040 kW. | Speed: 21.0 knots.

Passengers: 12. | Cabin Berths: 12.

Freight capacity: 2715 lane metres or 225 x 12m trailers.

Date of first sailing in Stena Line BV service: December 2010

Former names: *Stena Hispanica* (1998), *Sea Chieftain* (1998), *Stena Seafreighter* (2003)

Sister ship: *Stena Carrier, Ark Forwarder*

PRINCIPAL VESSELS USED BY STENA LINE BV ON THE HOOK–KILLINGHOLME ROUTE.

STENA TRADER (IMO: 9331177)

Built: 2005 the hull by Baltijsky Zavod Shipyard, Russia.

Equipped: 2006 at Fosen Mekaniske Verksted, Rissa, Norway - yard no.74.

Dimensions: 212.50 x 26.70 x 6.30 m. | Tonnage: 26660 gt.

Engines: Two MAN 9L48/60B diesels.

Power Output: 21600 kW. | Speed: 22.2 knots.

Passengers: 300. | Cabins: 100.

Cabin Berths: 204.

Freight capacity: 3100 lane metres or 250 x 12m trailers.

Date of first sailing in Stena Line BV service: 12th August 2006

Date of last day in service: 30th September 2010

Sister ship: *Stena Traveller*

STENA TRAVELLER (IMO: 9331189)

Built: 2006 the hull by Baltijsky Zavod Shipyard, Russia.

Equipped: 2007 at Fosen Mekaniske Verksted, Rissa, Norway - yard no.75.

Dimensions: 212.50 x 26.70 x 6.00 m.	Tonnage: 26660 gt.

Engines: Two MAN 9L48/60B diesels.

Power Output: 21600 kW.	Speed: 22.2 knots.
Passengers: 300.	Cabins: 100.

Cabin Berths: 204.

Freight capacity: 3100 lane metres or 250 x 12m trailers.

Date of first sailing in Stena Line BV service: 20th June 2007

Date of last day in service: December 2010. Still in service: as *Patria Seaways* with DFDS Seaways - Karlsham to Klaipeda (Baltic)

Sister ship: *Stena Trader*

CORAGGIO (IMO: 9350680)

Built: 2007 by Nuovi Cantieri Apuania Marina di Carrara, Italy - yard no.1237.

Dimensions: 199.14 x 26.60 x 6.40 m.	Tonnage: 24950 gt.

Engines: Two Wartsila 12V46 diesels.

Power Output: 24000 kW.	Speed: 24.0 knots.
Passengers: 500.	Cabin Berths: 268.

Freight capacity: 2623 lane metres or 215 x 12m trailers.

Date of first sailing in Stena Line BV service: 30th September 2010

Sister ships: *Audacia, Tenacia, Superfast I, Lisco Maxima, Superfast II, Forza, Energia*

FINNARROW (IMO: 9010814)

Built: 1996 by Pt Doc Kodja Bahri, Jakarta, Indonesia - yard no.1005.

Dimensions: 168.00 x 28.00 x 6.00 m.	Tonnage: 25996 gt.

Engines: Four Sulzer 6ZA40S diesels.

Power Output: 14700 kW.	Speed: 21.0 knots.
Passengers: 200.	Cabin Berths: 200.

Freight capacity: 2400 lane metres or 200 x 12m trailers.

Date of first sailing in Stena Line BV service: December 2010?

Former names: *Gotland*

New Stena Seabridger Class MkII

STENA TRANSPORTER (IMO:)

Built : 2011 by Samsung Yard, South Korea - yard no. 1807.

Dimensions: 212.00 x 26.70 x 6.30 m.	Tonnage: 34700 gt.

Engines: Two MAN diesels.

Power Output: 21600 kW.	Speed: -
Passengers: 300.	Cabin berths: 264.

Freight capacity: 4050 lane metres.

Date of first sailing in Stena Line BV service: February 2011

STENA TRANSIT (IMO:)

Built : 2011 by Samsung Yard, South Korea - yard no. 1808.

Dimensions: 212.00 x 26.70 x 6.30 m.	Tonnage: 34700 gt.

Engines: Two MAN diesels.

Power Output: 21600 kW.	Speed: -
Passengers: 300.	Cabin berths: 264.

Freight capacity: 4050 lane metres.

Date of first sailing in Stena Line BV service: October 2011

OTHER SHIPS

STENA TRAVELLER (IMO: 8917390)

Built: 1992 Bruce Shipyards, Landskrona, Equipped at Fosen FMV, Trondheim - yard no.51.

Dimensions: 154.00 x 24.33 x 5.90 m.	Tonnage: 18332 gt.

Engines: Two Wartsila Sulzer 8ZA40S diesel.

Power Output: 8980 kW.	Speed: 18.0 knots.
Passengers: 245.	Cabins: 88.

Freight capacity: 1800 lane metres

STENA SHIPPER (IMO: 7909621)

Built: 1979 Jos L Meyer Werft, Papenburg Ems, Germany - yard no.588.

Dimensions: 168.80 x 20.2 x 6.5 m.	Tonnage: 12237 gt.

Engines: One MAN 8L58/64 diesel.

Power Output: 11210 kW.	Speed: 17.0 knots.
Passengers: 12.	Cabin Berths: 12.

Freight capacity: 2080 lane metres

Scrapped, as *R. Shipper* after arriving at Alang on 29th November 2011.

AMANDA (IMO: 7729045)

Built: 1978 Paul Lindenau Werft, Kiel, Germany - yard no.177.

Dimensions: 172.90 x 21.37x 7.56 m.	Tonnage: 14715 gt.

Engines: Two MAK 9M551AK diesel.

Power Output: 11604 kW.	Speed: 14.5 knots.
Passengers: 12.	Cabin Berths: 12.

Freight capacity: 1810 lane metres or 133 x 12m trailers

Scrapped, after arriving at Alang on 20th March 2010.

FLEET LIST UPDATE 2020

Principal vessels used by Stena Line BV on the Hook-Killingholme route.

STENA TRADER (IMO: 9331177)

Built: 2005 the hull by Baltijsky Zavod Shipyard, Russia.

Equipped: 2006 at Fosen Mekaniske Verksted, Rissa, Norway - yard no.74.

Dimensions: 212.50 x 26.70 x 6.30 m.	Tonnage: 26660 gt.
Engines: Two MAN 9L48/60B diesels.	Power Output: 21600 kW.
Speed: 22.2 knots.	
Passengers: 300. Cabins: 100.	Cabin Berths: 204.

Freight capacity: 3100 lane metres or 250 x 12m trailers.

Date of first sailing in Stena Line BV service: 12th August 2006

Date of last day in service: 30th September 2010

Sister ship: *Stena Traveller*

STENA TRAVELLER (IMO: 9331189)

Built: 2006 the hull by Baltijsky Zavod Shipyard, Russia.

Equipped: 2007 at Fosen Mekaniske Verksted, Rissa, Norway - yard no.75.

Dimensions: 212.50 x 26.70 x 6.00 m.	Tonnage: 26660 gt.

Above: The **Bora Bay** *was chartered by Stena Line in 2019. (Rob de Visser)*

Right: *A powerful view of the* **Stena Forerunner** *in the New Waterway. (Rob de Visser)*

Right: *The chartered* **Qezban** *entered service on the Rotterdam freight link in March 2020. (Rob de Visser)*

Engines: Two MAN 9L48/60B diesels. Power Output: 21600 kW. Speed: 22.2 knots.

Passengers: 300. Cabins: 100. Cabin Berths: 204.

Freight capacity: 3100 lane metres or 250 x 12m trailers.

Date of first sailing in Stena Line BV service: 20th June 2007

Date of last day in service: 10th December 2010

Sister ship: *Stena Trader*

CORAGGIO (IMO: 9350680)

Built: 2007 by Nuovi Cantieri Apuania Marina di Carrara, Italy - yard no.1237.

Dimensions: 199.14 x 26.60 x 6.40 m. Tonnage: 24950 gt.

Engines: Two Wartsila 12V46 diesels. Power Output: 24000 kW. Speed: 24.0 knots.

Passengers: 500. Cabin Berths: 268.

Freight capacity: 2623 lane metres or 215 x 12m trailers.

Date of first sailing in Stena Line BV service: 30th September 2010

Date of last day in service: 7th November 2011

Names since leaving Stena Line BV: *Athena Seaways* (2013)

Sister ships: *Audacia*, *Tenacia*, *Superfast I*, *Lisco Maxima*, *Superfast II*, *Forza*, *Energia*

FINNARROW (IMO: 9010814)

Built: 1996 by Pt Dok Kodja Bahri, Jakarta, Indonesia - yard no.1005.

Dimensions: 168.00 x 28.00 x 6.00 m. Tonnage: 25996 gt.

Engines: Four Sulzer 6ZA40S diesels. Power Output: 14700 kW. Speed: 21.0 knots.

Passengers: 200. Cabin Berths: 200.

Freight capacity: 2400 lane metres or 200 x 12m trailers.

Date of first sailing in Stena Line BV service: 10th December 2010

Date of last day in service: 1st March 2011

Former names: *Gotland* (1996), *Finnarrow* (1997).

Names since leaving Stena Line BV: *Euroferry Brindisi* (2013), *Mazovia* (2014).

New Stena Seabridger Class MkII

STENA TRANSPORTER (IMO: 9469376)

Built: 2011 by Samsung Heavy Industries, Geoje Shipyard, South Korea - yard no. 1807.

Dimensions: 212.00 x 26.70 x 6.30 m. Tonnage: 34700 gt.

Engines: Two STX-MAN 9L 48/60B diesels. Power Output: 21600 kW. Speed: 22.0 knots.

Passengers: 300. Cabin berths: 264.

Freight capacity: 4050 lane metres or 260 freight units.

Date of first sailing in Stena Line BV service: 1st March 2011

STENA TRANSIT (IMO: 9469388)

Built: 2011 by Samsung Heavy Industries, Geoje Shipyard, South Korea - yard no. 1808.

Dimensions: 212.00 x 26.70 x 6.30 m. Tonnage: 34700 gt.

Engines: Two STX-MAN 9L 48/60B diesels. Power Output: 21600 kW. Speed: 22.0 knots.

Passengers: 300. Cabin berths: 264.

Freight capacity: 4050 lane metres or 260 freight units.

Date of first sailing in Stena Line BV service: 7th November 2011

Principal vessels used by Stena Line BV on the Harwich-Rotterdam route.

STENA CARRIER (IMO: 9138800)

Built: 1998 by Societa Esercizio Cantieri S.p.A, Viareggio, Italy - yard no. 1548.

Dimensions: 182.60 x 25.50 x 7.40 m. Tonnage: 21104 gt.

Engines: Four Sulzer 8ZA40S diesels. Power Output: 23040 kW. Speed: 21.0 knots.

Passengers: 12. Cabin Berths: 12.

Freight capacity: 2715 lane metres or 225 x 12m trailers.

Date of first sailing in Stena Line BV service: 6th September 2010

Date of last day in service: 3rd September 2012

Former names: *Aronte* (1998), *Stena Carrier II (*2004), *Stena Carrier* (2004).

Names since leaving Stena Line BV: Mexico Star (2018).

Sister ships: *Stena Freighter*, *Ark Forwarder*

ARK FORWARDER (IMO: 9138783)

Built: 1998 by Societa Esercizio Cantieri S.p.A, Viareggio, Italy - yard no. 1546.

Dimensions: 182.60 x 25.50 x 7.40 m. Tonnage: 21104 gt.

Engines: Four Sulzer 8ZA40S diesels. Power Output: 23040 kW. Speed: 21.0 knots.

Passengers: 12. Cabin Berths: 12.

Freight capacity: 2715 lane metres or 225 x 12m trailers.

Date of first sailing in Stena Line BV service: 20th December 2010

Date of last day in service: 26th April 2011

Former names: *Stena Ausonia* (1998), *Sea Centurion* (1998), *Mont Ventoux* (2003), *Stena Forwarder* (2005), *Ark Forwarder* (2007).

Names since leaving Stena Line BV: *Wilhelmsborg* (2015), *Ark Forwarder* (2016), *MSC Bridge* (2018).

Sister ships: *Stena Carrier*, *Stena Freighter*.

STENA FREIGHTER (IMO: 9138795)

Built: 1998 by Societa Esercizio Cantieri S.p.A, Viareggio, Italy - yard no. 1547.

Dimensions: 182.60 x 25.50 x 7.40 m. Tonnage: 21104 gt.

Engines: Four Sulzer 8ZA40S diesels. Power Output: 23040 kW. Speed: 21.0 knots.

Passengers: 12. Cabin Berths: 12.

Freight capacity: 2715 lane metres or 225 x 12m trailers.

Date of first sailing in Stena Line BV service: 26th April 2011

Date of last day in service: 31st August 2012

Former names: *Stena Hispanica* (1997), *Sea Chieftain* (1998), *Stena Seafreighter* (2003), *Stena Freighter* (2004).

Names since leaving Stena Line BV: LPV (2018).

Sister ships: *Stena Carrier*, *Ark Forwarder*

CAPUCINE (IMO: 9539066)

Built: 2011 by Kyokuyo Shipbuilding & Iron Works, Shimonoseki, Japan - yard no. 500.

Dimensions: 152.00 x 22.00 x 5.40 m. Tonnage: 16342 gt.

Engines: One Wartsila 12V32 diesel. Power Output: 7000 kW. Speed: 17.5 knots.

Passengers: 12. Cabin Berths: 12.

Freight capacity: 1760 metres or 160 freight units.

Date of first sailing in Stena Line BV service: 3rd September 2012

Date of last day in service: December 2017

Sister ships: Severine, Wilhelmine, Adeline.

SEVERINE (IMO: 9539078)

Built: 2012 by Kyokuyo Shipbuilding & Iron Works, Shimonoseki, Japan - yard no. 501

Dimensions: 152.00 x 22.00 x 5.40 m.	Tonnage: 16342 gt.
Engines: One Wartsila 12V32 diesel.	Power Output: 7000 kW. Speed: 17.5 knots.
Passengers: 12. Cabin Berths: 12.	

Freight capacity: 1760 metres or 160 freight units.

Date of first sailing in Stena Line BV service: 3rd September 2012

Date of last day in service: December 2017

Sister ships: Capucine, *Wilhelmine, Adeline.*

STENA FORERUNNER (IMO: 9227259)

Built: 2003 by Dalian Shipyard, Dalian, China - yard no. ro123-3.

Dimensions: 195.30 x 26.80 x 6.60 m.	Tonnage: 24688 gt.
Engines: Four Sulzer 8ZAL40S diesels.	Power Output: 24000 kW. Speed: 22.5 knots
Passengers: 12. Cabin Berths: 12.	

Freight capacity: 3000 lane metres or 210 x 13m trailers.

Date of first sailing in Stena Line BV service: 12th January 2018 (Harwich - Rotterdam until June 2018, Rotterdam - Killingholme from March 2019 - March 2020, then Harwich - Rotterdam)

Sister ships: *Stena Foreteller, Stena Forecaster.*

MISTRAL (IMO: 9183788)

Built: 1998 by J.J. Sietas, Hamburg, Germany - yard no. 1183.

Dimensions: 153.45 x 20.60 x 7.00 m.	Tonnage: 10471 gt.
Engines: One Wartsila 12V46B diesel.	Power Output: 12600 kW. Speed: 22.0 knots.
Passengers: 12. Cabin Berths: 12.	

 Freight capacity: 1625 lane metres or 102 trailers.

Date of first sailing in Stena Line BV service: 2nd June 2018

Last day in service: 21st August 2018

Sister ships: *Caroline Russ, Elisabeth Russ, Friedrich Russ, Miranda, Pauline Russ, Seagard.*

BORE BAY (IMO: 9122007)

Built: 1996 by Umoe Sterkoder A.S., Kristiansund, Norway - yard no.150.

Dimensions: 138.50 x 22.70 x 7.10 m.	Tonnage: 10572 gt.
Engines: One Wartsila 16V46 diesel.	Power Output:

14480 kW.	Speed: 20.0 knots.
Passengers: 12.	Cabin Berths: 12.

Freight capacity: 1511 lane metres or 116 x 12m trailers.

Date of first sailing in Stena Line BV service: 19th August 2018

Last day in service: 26th February 2019

Former names: *Heralden* (1996), *Auto Bay* (2007), *Bore Bay* (2017).

Sister ships: *Serenaden, Transgard.*

SOMERSET (IMO: 9188221)

Built: 2000 by Flender Werft, Lubeck, Germany - yard no. 676.

Dimensions: 183.40 x 25.20 x 7.50 m.	Tonnage: 21005 gt.
Engines: One Sulzer 7RTA52U diesel.	Power Output: 10920 kW. Speed: 18.0 knots.
Passengers: 12. Cabin Berths: 12.	

Freight capacity: 2475 lane metres or 190 x 12m trailers.

Date of first sailing in Stena Line BV service: 19th September 2018

Former names: *Spaarneborg* (2000), *Somerset* (2015).

Sister ships: *Schieborg, Slingeborg*

STENA NORDICA (IMO: 9215505)

Built: 2000 by Mitsubishi Heavy Industries, Shimonoseki, Japan - yard no.1068.

Dimensions: 170.51 x 25.82 x 6.00 m.	Tonnage: 24206 gt.
Engines: Two Wartsila 18V38 diesels and Two Wartsila 12V38 diesels. Power Output: 39600 kW.	Speed: 25.7 knots.
Passengers: 405. Cabin Berths: 222.	

Freight capacity: 1949 lane metres or 122 x 12m trailers.

Date of first sailing in Stena Line BV service: 13th January 2020

Last day in service: 22nd January 2020

Former names: *European Ambassador* (2000), *Stena Nordica* (2004), *Malo Seaways* (2015), *Stena Nordica* (2016).

Principal vessels used by Stena Line BV on the Rotterdam - Killingholme route.

STENA SCOTIA (IMO: 9121625)

Built: 1996 by Miho Shipyard, Shimizu, China - yard no.1459.

Dimensions: 142.50 x 23.20 x 5.40 m.	Tonnage: 13017 gt.
Engines: Two Sulzer 8ZAV40S diesels.	Power Output: 9000 kW. Speed: 18.0 knots.
Passengers: 12. Cabin Berths: 12.	

*The **Hatche** coming astern at Europoort shortly after her starting her charter with Stena Line in January 2020. (Rob de Visser)*

The **Misida** *is seen here at the Hook of Holland loading for Killingholme with* **Stena Transit***. (Rob de Visser)*

Freight capacity: 1562 lane metres or 110 x 12m trailers.

Date of first sailing in Stena Line BV service: 2nd September 2014 (Rotterdam - Killingholme until 4th January 2018, then Rotterdam - Harwich)

Date of last day in service: mid August 2018

Former names: *Maersk Exporter* (1996), *Scotia Seaways* (2010), *Stena Scotia* (2011).

Sister ships: *Maersk Importer, Maersk Anglia, Maersk Flander*s.

CAROLINE RUSS (IMO: 9197533)

Built: 1999 by J.J. Sietas KG, Hamburg, Germany - yard no.1188.

Dimensions: 153.45 x 20.60 x 7.00 m.	Tonnage: 10488 gt.
Engines: One Wartsila 16V64B diesel. 11030 kW. Speed: 21.0 knots.	Power Output:
Passengers: 12. Cabin Berths: 12	

Freight capacity: 1624 lane metres or 102 x 12m trailers.

Date of first sailing in Stena Line BV service: 31st October 2016

Date of last day in service: 4th January 2018

Former names: *Caroline Russ* (1999), *Corsica Linea Dui* (2016), *Caroline Russ* (2016).

Sister ships: *Elisabeth Russ, Friedrich Russ, Mistral, Miranda, Pauline Russ, Seagard.*

MISANA (IMO: 9348936)

Built: 2007 by J.J. Sietas, Hamburg, Germany - yard no.1281.

Dimensions: 165.75 x 23.40 x 7.26 m.	Tonnage: 15586 gt.
Engines: Two Wartsila 6L46F diesels. 15000 kW. Speed: 20.0 knots.	Power Output:
Passengers: 12. Cabin Berths: 12.	

Freight capacity: 2133 lane metres or 158 x 12m trailers.

Date of first sailing in Stena Line BV service: 4th January 2018

Date of last day in service: early March 2020.

Sister ship: *Misida* .

MISIDA (IMO: 9348948)

Built: 2007 by J.J. Sietas, Hamburg, Germany - yard no.1282.

Dimensions: 165.75 x 23.40 x 7.26 m.	Tonnage: 15586 gt.
Engines: Two Wartsila 6L46F diesels. 15000 kW. Speed: 20.0 knots.	Power Output:
Passengers: 12. Cabin Berths: 12.	

Freight capacity: 2133 lane metres or 158 x 12m trailers.

Date of first sailing in Stena Line BV service: 4th January 2018

Date of last day in service: end January 2020.

Sister ship: *Misana*

HATCHE (IMO: 9457165)

Built: 2009 by Odense Staalskibsvaerft A/S, Odense, Denmark - yard no.217.

Dimensions: 193.00 x 26.00 x 6.50 m.	Tonnage: 29004 gt.
Engines: Two MaK 9M43 diesels. 16200 kW. Speed: 21.5 knots.	Power Output:
Passengers: 12. Cabin Berths: 12.	

Freight capacity: 3663 lane metres or 240 trailers.

Date of first sailing in Stena Line BV service: 28th January 2020

Former names: *Maas Viking* (2009), *Kent* (2012), *Hatche* (2013).

Sister ships: *Wessex, Humber Viking, Mercia, Cragside, Strait of Messina, Strait of Magellan, Bering Strait.*

QEZBAN (IMO: 9457189)

Built: 2010 by Odense Staalskibsvaerft A/S, Odense, Denmark - yard no.219.

Dimensions: 193.00 x 26.00 x 6.50 m.	Tonnage: 28870 gt.
Engines: Two MaK 9M43 diesels. 16200 kW. Speed: 21.5 knots.	Power Output:
Passengers: 12. Cabin Berths: 12.	

Freight capacity: 3663 lane metres or 240 trailers.

Date of first sailing in Stena Line BV service: 8th March 2020

Former names: *Wessex* (2010), *Qezban* (2013).

Sister ships: *Maas Viking, Humber Viking, Mercia, Cragside, Strait of Messina, Strait of Magellan, Bering Strait.*

Principal vessels used by Stena Line BV on the Harwich - Hook route.

STENA HIBERNIA (IMO: 9121637)

Built: 1996 by Miho Shipyard, Shimizu, China - yard no.1460.

Dimensions: 142.50 x 23.47 x 5.40 m.	Tonnage: 13017 gt.
Engines: Two Sulzer 8ZAV40S diesels. kW. Speed: 18.0 knots.	Power Output: 9000
Passengers: 12. Cabin Berths: 12.	

Freight capacity: 1562 lane metres or 110 x 12m trailers.

Date of first sailing in Stena Line BV service: 29th September 2012

Date of last day in service: 10th October 2012

Former names: *Maersk Importer* (1996), *Hibernia Seaways* (2010), *Stena Hibernia* (2011).

Sister ships: *Maersk Exporter, Maersk Anglia, Maersk Flanders.*